Donated by the Pollack Family

לעלוי נשמת

יעקב שמעון פאללאק ז"ל

in memory of

Yaacov Shimon Pollack Z.L

*Bayis Ne'eman b'Yisrael*

FELDHEIM PUBLISHERS
*Jerusalem & New York*

# *Bayis Ne'eman b'Yisrael*

## practical steps to success in marriage

### DR. MEIR WIKLER

First published 1988

Hardcover edition: ISBN 0-87306-458-5
Paperback edition: ISBN 0-87306-464-x

Philipp Feldheim Inc.
200 Airport Executive Park
Spring Valley, NY 10977

Feldheim Publishers Ltd.
POB 6525 / Jerusalem, Israel

Printed in Israel

*R. Yitzchak said: "If someone tells you,*
*'I toiled but did not find,' do not believe him;*
*'I did not toil but I found,' do not believe him;*
*'I toiled and I found,' then you should believe*
*him." (Megilla 6b)*

ב"ה

היער והבהירות אל בויינא שליעבם ישלוחם בזאמצל יקרת
רגשון בקרייתו עם סיולי והקפים כבוד הרב שליצמרי שיפר
עובדים אל היום בזה הגיוזע חובבים לאתישיבן כני
שויגורי ואגלו זמזן וענאבים נסיונות התמד שתם עוד
קיימת אתכי והיגל עמזבות חיי שלום לכין שאני
שגזילו שגזלה עד מזא, ולא עם נשאני שלו של חאי
גברא יקירו יוזל יביבי הגזזה מאיך אלי' ויקלך שהנ
שפקיד שם ואתישלה יגל להחר שי' חשא וזמזל
חולף על שינין' בויינ ושלום ביה כיזד שואהי וזירה
וענזיב ינשף ה' ביב פלין שתני מפר ילזא כזואתיה
לגיזן הדרכים והזינים בנעשב ילד לשא! כבל הליכות
התם וליזיק ליזה ליצור הביה שלום וריזבי ולזיתו
שתכן ובית גלקהם יסתלו שבו זשלים ושא שתה
בזעק בלל וזיל.

יזיז בושאזם בג יום לחולזל אבר תשא
פה בבוקלטן אפ/00.
השבויה גל ישרת השנ ולבזות קרן ישראל.

**CONGREGATION BETH PINCHAS • NEW ENGLAND CHASSIDIC CENTER**
**GRAND RABBI LEVI I. HOROWITZ** • בית המדרש בית פינחס של אדמו"ר מבאסטאן
**1710 BEACON STREET • BROOKLINE, MASS. 02146 • RE 4 5100**

(The following is a free translation of the Rebbe's letter.)

Since the problems related to *shidduchim* are well known, as our Sages of Blessed Memory have stated, "Making matches is as difficult as splitting the Red Sea," (*Sota* 2a); and especially in this generation where even after passing through the turbulent sea of *shidduchim* couples find that the tribulations of life continue; and since harmony and peace between husband and wife are extremely vital, Dr. Meir Wikler has written a very important and urgently needed *saifer* on matters of *shalom bayis* for the Torah community.

I know him to be an expert in guiding people along the proper path in life and in advising how to adorn the home with peace, making it a sanctuary and house of God and thereby meriting true peace to dwell among *klal Yisrael*.

The Bostoner Rebbe, Grand Rabbi Levi I. Horowitz
24th day of Adar, 5747
Brookline, Mass.

Rabbi CHAIM P. SCHEINBERG

KIRYAT MATTERSDORF

PANIM MEIROT 2

JERUSALEM, ISRAEL

הרב חיים פנחס שיינברג

ראש ישיבת "תורה אור"

ומורה הוראה דקרית מטרסדורף

ירושלים טל.ג1ג131ג5

The saifer Bayis Ne'eman B'Yisrael is geared for young men and women of marriageable age. It contains practical advice, presented in a clear, direct and easy-to-read format, which answers the most common questions regarding dating, courtship and marriage. Many of the problems which interfere with shalom bayis are also discussed, along with specific suggestions for avoiding them. This saifer, then, includes some of the most important guidance young men and women need in order to establish their marriages upon a solid foundation of shalom bayis.

The author is a qualified professional who has drawn extensively upon his own clinical experience counseling hundreds of couples. The numerous case histories which appear throughout the saifer will enable everyone to relate to the hadracha on a personal level. In addition, the author draws heavily upon his Torah hashkafa which is clearly evidenced, as well. In short, the author is a true ben Torah and it is clear from this saifer that his yiras shamayim has not been compromised by his professionalism.

Our generation today is witness to far too many marital breakdowns which cause untold pain and trauma to all parties involved. Any means of reducing or eliminating these personal tragedies must be embraced enthusiastically. Since this saifer provides sound guidance on Torah family life, it should be read by all young men and women prior to marriage. It should also be read by parents and rebbeim who want to be sure they are doing everything they can to help prepare their children and talmidim for marriage.

Hopefully, this saifer will be circulated widely and read extensively so that the marriages of tomorrow will stand the greatest chances of achieving and maintaining shalom bayis.

Chaim P. Scheinberg

Erev Rosh Chodesh Elul, 5747

**THE JEWISH OBSERVER**

A Journal of Jewish Thought

4 Adar, 5748

February 22, 1988

The Jewish family is the cornerstone of our people, the primary means of transmitting our heritage from generation to generation. If the family is in trouble, it is a crisis situation for our people, to say the least.

The Jewish family <u>is</u> in trouble, judging by the rising frequency of divorces in our community. All the more reason why I welcome the appearance of Dr. Meir Wikler's excellent book, "Bayis Ne'man B'Yisrael: Practical Steps to Success in Marriage," which deals with heading off problems of Shalom Bayis -- domestic harmony -- before they strike.

Dr. Wikler's common-sense approach, based on Torah values and years of solid front-line experience, expressed in clear understandable prose, is a worthy contribution to both individual need and -- yes -- national welfare.

Rabbi Nisson Wolpin, Editor

<u>The Jewish Observer</u>

BROOKLYN LAW SCHOOL
250 JORALEMON STREET
BROOKLYN, NEW YORK 11201

AARON D. TWERSKI
PROFESSOR OF LAW

AREA CODE 718
625-2200

My chaver and chavrusa, Dr. Meir Wikler, has written a sensitive and sensible book for those embarking upon dating and marriage. It should be read by young men and women and should be studied by parents whose children have reached the age of shidduchim. This book is not intended to be a psychologist's treatise on the subject. It does, however, identify with great clarity many of the problems which tend to repeat themselves with such frightening regularity. In this book's pages I see before me many couples whose marriages came to a tragic end. They need not have come to such a conclusion. No one recognized the problems early enough to make wise and discriminating choices. Hopefully the straightforward approach set forth herein will help reduce the terrible trauma and pain that attend the destruction of shalom bayis.

When facing the problems of shalom bayis we are wont to say that the problems are so rampant because we have learned to imitate the non-Jewish world. Azoi vee se kriselt sich azoi yidelt sich. And this is of course true. There are, however, problems that do not stem primarily from the non-Jewish world. Some have a decidedly frum Jewish twist to them. Parental interference has, in my opinion, become a frum Jewish art from. It gnaws away at marriages like a cancer. This is especially true in the case of young marriages and parents who provide financial support. It is rather clear that young marriages will not disappear. Both for halachic and social reasons they will be the rule. But the need for parents to understand the dynamics of their relationship with their married children cannot be overstated. Dr. Wikler treats the subject with insight and caring. If anything, I would take a harsher view than he. My experience teaches me that parents must learn to stay out of the children's way. Any parental involvement should be undertaken only after full consultation with a gadol b'Yisrael. Pikuach Nefesh demands the psak halacha of the greatest Torah scholars of the age.

Some will say that there is nothing startling or new in this book. That may be so. But when truths are so eloquently and simply stated, it is time for rejoicing. Those who will read it will come away with a heightened sense of awareness. They will be able to express in words and deed that which they may have only dimly perceived. And that is a great accomplishment indeed.

Rosh Chodesh Menachem Av
5747

Aaron Twerski

*Bayis Ne'eman b'Yisrael*

# Contents

# Acknowledgments

*Baruch HaShem* I have merited the opportunity to have met, learned with and been guided by some of the most outstanding *rebbe'im*, *rabbanim* and *roshai yeshiva* of our time. In addition, I was privileged to have been taught, supervised and trained by the most talented professors and clinical supervisors anyone could want. Furthermore, I have been fortunate to have worked consistently alongside high-caliber colleagues from whom I have also learned a great deal.

It would be an overwhelming and nearly impossible task, therefore, for me to list everyone from whom I have learned and benefited. Nevertheless, I am truly grateful to them all, and I hope that they will accept this, albeit collective, expression of appreciation.

I would, however, like to thank the following people who have directly contributed their comments, suggestions and advice at various stages during the development of this book.

*HaGa'on HaRav* Avrohom Pam, *shlita, Rosh Yeshiva* of Yeshiva Torah Voda'ath, for his most generous permission to include his essay, "The Jewish Home: Mainstay of Our People," as the introductory essay of this book and for his invaluable, critical readings of the manuscript;

Grand Rabbi Levi I. Horowitz, the Bostoner Rebbe, *shlita,* for his constructive criticism of the manuscript and for his kind and laudatory letter of approbation;

Grand Rabbi Yaakov Perlow, the Novominsker Rebbe, *shlita,* for his helpful comments on earlier versions of chapters 3, 4 and 6;

*HaGa'on HaRav* Chaim P. Scheinberg, *shlita, Rosh Hayeshiva,* Yeshiva Torah Ore and *Morah D'asra,* Kiryat Mattersdorf, for reviewing the manuscript and for his generous letter of approbation;

*HaRav* Dovid Cohen, *shlita, Morah D'asra,* Congregation Gevul Yavitz, for his critical reading of the manuscript and for his enthusiastic letter of approbation;

Rabbi Nisson Wolpin, editor of the *Jewish Observer,* for his expert editorial input on earlier versions of chapters 1, 2, 3, 4 and 6, for permission to reprint *HaRav* Pam's article, which originally appeared in the *Jewish Observer,* for reviewing the final draft of the manuscript and for his gracious letter of approbation;

Rabbi Yosef Wikler, *Menahel* of Yeshiva Birkas Reuven and editor of *Kashrus Magazine*, for reviewing the manuscript and for his fraternal advice and counsel;

Rabbi Dr. Aaron D. Twerski, Professor of Law, Brooklyn Law School, for his practical suggestions and for his eloquent letter of approbation;

Messrs. Yaakov and Yitzchok Feldheim, editors at Feldheim Publishers, for their vote of confidence in accepting this book for publication and for their excellent editorial guidance;

Yaakov Salomon, C.S.W., close friend and colleague, for his thorough critiques of the manuscript at various stages and for his continuous, enthusiastic encouragement along the way;

A *chabura* (close-knit group) of *rabbanim*, *mechanchim* (educators), and *mashgichim* (deans of students in yeshivos) who have all chosen to remain anonymous. The *chabura* has met with me two or three times each summer since 1982 to discuss the problems of their *talmidim* and *talmidos*, mostly related to dating, courtship and marriage. These meetings have been a source of tremendous inspiration for me, and I have received the strongest appeal from the *chabura* to write this book.

"*Achron, achron chaviv*"(the best is saved for last), my dear wife, Malka, *shetichyeh*, for her faithful support and patient indulgence throughout my career for which she deserves *at least* half the credit for whatever I have been able to accomplish *b'ezras HaShem*. Of her it may be said, "That which is mine and that which is yours all comes from her" (*Kesubos* 63a).

# Preface

The fact that 50% of all American marriages end in divorce is such common knowledge today that authors and social scientists no longer find it necessary to cite authoritative sources when they refer to this statistic.

*Baruch HaShem* the rate of divorce in the Orthodox Jewish community is much lower than that of the larger American society. The exact rate of Orthodox divorce cannot, and perhaps should not, be measured, because such statistics could be easily misused. Nevertheless, most of us would agree that the rate is much too high.

Concern for the rate of divorce even among the *bnai Torah* leads parents, educators and young people themselves to search for the root causes of divorce in the Torah community. Certainly, there is no single factor that is responsible for the family breakdowns in our community. Each divorce can be traced to many complex societal and personality factors, and simple answers to complex questions are worthless.

But there does seem to be one factor which crops up with increasing frequency, not only in cases of divorce but also with married couples for whom *shalom bayis* (marital harmony) has become an elusive dream. That factor is a lack of adequate preparation for marriage on the part of the husband, the wife or both.

The purpose of this book, then, is to help you prepare for your marriage. If you are already married, perhaps this book can help you prepare for the rest of your married life. Whether you are standing at the threshold of marriage or whether you have crossed that threshold many years ago, it is hoped that you will be able to learn from the mistakes of others which are illustrated throughout this book, with actual case histories and vignettes.

There are many critical materials and components required to build a solid house, and you need not be a contractor to realize that one of the most important components of any house is the foundation. So since every house is built to last, careful consideration is always given to the design and construction of the foundation.

Your marriage will rest (or already rests) on the foundation of your preparation. But how many of us actively, deliberately and consciously prepare for marriage nowadays? Much more time, effort and money is invested in preparing for the first few hours of marriage (the wedding) than is invested in preparing for marriage itself.

So why not invest the time, now, to read this short book as part of your preparation plan to construct a solid foundation for your marriage? If you do, you may be able to strengthen that foundation and thereby insure that the marital house erected on that foundation will become a true *bayis ne'eman b'Yisrael* (an everlasting Jewish home).

# Foreword to Parents and Educators

As HaRav Avrohom Pam, *shlita*, points out in his introductory essay, "The Jewish Home: Mainstay of Our People," you play an important role in preparing young people for marriage. Ideally, therefore, they should turn to you for guidance and direction in preparing themselves for marriage. You have an ongoing relationship with them, and as a result, you understand their individual needs, strengths and weaknesses. In addition, you have a wealth of personal experience and knowledge of *Toras habayis* (Torah sources relating to marriage and family life) on which to base your advice and counsel. Finally, you approach the awesome task of preparing young people for marriage with a depth of compassionate, sincere concern which is unmatched by friends or other relatives.

In spite of all the good reasons for young people to consult with you in preparation for marriage, they do not always choose to do so. In such cases, these young people are quite bereft of the vital guidance they need in order to insure a successful journey through married life.

One of the purposes of this book, therefore, is to provide premarital guidance for those young people who will not take advantage of the guidance which you are so ready and eager to offer. In fact, one theme which is unabashedly repeated throughout this book is the overt encouragement to young people to reach out to you for your guidance.

Of course, not all parents and *mechanchim* are equally trained and experienced in counseling young people. Just as being a *talmid chacham* does not automatically make someone a successful yeshiva *rebbe*, so, too, understanding the complexities of married life does not guarantee that someone will be able to effectively counsel young people planning marriage. Young people often have many difficult and challenging questions which are not at all easy to answer.

So a second purpose of this book is to provide *supplemental* guidelines to those young people who do consult with you, since there may be some questions you are not equipped to answer or some questions they do not feel comfortable raising with you. If these young people find any contradictions between the advice contained here and that which you are providing, hopefully they will raise these points with you. Then you will have the opportunity to engage them in further discussion of the relevant issues.

Although this book is addressed to the young people themselves, it is hoped that you will read it as well. The book contains many case illustrations drawn from the author's clinical experience in counseling hundreds of married and separated couples, divorced individuals and single people experiencing difficulty with some aspect of *shidduchim*, dating or engagement. These case examples have been gleaned from over fifteen years of clinical practice in the Orthodox and Chassidic communities. As a result, this book is based on the kind of first-hand experience which some of you do not have.

The third purpose of this book, then, is to provide you with a launching pad for your own discussions with young people about marriage. Certainly, this book does not contain everything you need to know in order to effectively prepare young people for marriage. Only *Shas* (the entire *Talmud*) contains that. But this book can serve as an outline of topics you may want to cover with your sons, daughters and *talmidim*. In addition, this book will offer you the unique perspective of listening behind the door of a marriage counselor's office. Finally, this book can provide suggestions to you for responding to some of the most formidable questions you may ever encounter.

To summarize, this book has been written with a threefold purpose. First, it is designed to provide premarital guidance to those young people who cannot or will not discuss these matters with you. Secondly, this book is addressed to young people who do consult with you and who can benefit from additional preparatory guidance. Thirdly, this book is written for you, in order to serve as an additional shoulder to lighten what HaRav Pam, *shlita*, referred to as your "burden of prevention." (p. 30)

May we soon merit the lightening of all our burdens with the advent of *Mashiach Tzidkainu, bimhaira biyamainu, Amen.*

Meir Wikler, D.S.W.
Brooklyn, New York.
תשמ"ח/5748

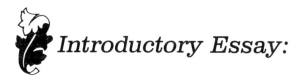

# Introductory Essay:

The following essay is based on remarks by HaRav Avrohom Pam, *shlita*, *rosh yeshiva* of Mesivta Torah Vodaath, at a gathering of his students. While the words are addressed to the "men of the house," with little change, they can be a source of guidance and enlightenment to women as well.

This essay first appeared in the *Jewish Observer* (Summer 1982) and is reprinted here with the permission of HaRav Pam, *shlita*, and the editor of the *Jewish Observer*.

## The Jewish Home: Mainstay of Our People

Everyone strives to be successful in life, with varying degrees of effort, depending upon how important the particular endeavor is to him. Of highest priority to most people is achievement in business or the profession of one's choice, and it is to this that he applies his utmost. The development of a happy, solid family life is not often given that much effort, for it is not understood to be so notable an achievement. Yet a home where the husband and wife are devoted to each other and live in harmony, where the spiritual growth and Torah development of the children is a dominant concern — such a house is a מקדש מעט, a sanctuary in miniature, where the *Sh'china* dwells. Creation of such a house represents a true mark of success, a goal to strive for, an accomplishment in which to take justifiable pride. Since *shalom bayis* problems — problems of domestic strife — seem to abound, it would seem that, unfortunately, people do not recognize the value of this achievement.

### THE CORNERSTONE

The cornerstone is mutual love and respect, תוכו רצוף אהבה, "Full of love within." / And, like any aspect of a life lived according to the Torah, it is guided by the dictum: דרכיה דרכי נועם, "Its ways are ways of pleasantness."

As a frame of reference, one should, from time to time, ask himself why his *neshama* was dispatched from celestial spheres to this world — certainly not to make other people miserable or to be a thorn in his wife's side. Surely the Divine gift of life was not meant to be abused this way. To underscore the importance of mutual respect in marriage and to understand the full import of that concept, note the admonition of the *Maggid* to the *Bais Yosef*.

The *Maggid* — that is, the heavenly emissary that regularly visited with the *Bais Yosef* (Rabbi Yosef Caro, the author of the *Shulchan Aruch*) — once revealed to the *Bais Yosef* the sacred essence of his wife's *neshama*.* He then explained why he did so: "So you may appreciate her and honor her accordingly." One may be certain that the *Bais Yosef* followed to the letter all the *halachos* spelled out in the *Shulchan Aruch* in regard to "Love your wife as yourself and honor her more than yourself." Yet the *Maggid* felt that with a greater awareness of the lofty nature of his wife's *neshama*, the *Bais Yosef*'s respect for her would be enhanced even further.

We are not worthy of visitations by *Maggidim*, to

---

* See *Maggid Mesharim: Parshas Va'aira*

reveal cosmic secrets to us, but in the World-to-Come we may be shocked to discover who really was the gift of God to be our partner in life. Imagine a person's shame when he will realize the sublime soul his wife possessed, and he will recall the careless or even abusive manner in which he treated her during their years together! But then it will be too late to do anything about it.

One really does not have to wait for heavenly emissaries or for other-worldly revelations for an indication of the sanctity of the *neshama* of the women in today's Torah society. Thoroughly imbued with the values taught in the Bais Yaakov schools and seminaries, they are guided by a loving commitment to a life of Torah and a desire to serve *Klal Yisrael* by raising a family loyal to Torah. The mere fact that a woman can entertain and nurture such feelings in the midst of a society that is so depraved and void of sanctity is of itself an indication of the lofty stature of her soul. Such a woman surely merits honor for her own sake!

## THE ROUTE TO SHALOM BAYIS

*Shalom bayis* is not to be taken for granted and left to run its own course. Like a beautiful garden it needs constant care and concern. It is interesting that in the *Kesuba* (marriage contract), the husband pledges: ואנא אפלח ואוקיר ואיזון ואפרנס יתיכי ליכי... "I will work, honor, feed, and support you." It would seem that the promise to honor is out of order, for it should have been placed first: "honor, work, feed, and support you." The fact that "work" is first would seem to indicate that just as supporting one's wife calls for a great investment of time and effort, so too must one

work at properly honoring her. It is an aspect of life
that does not take care of itself, but can suffer seriously
if neglected.

Being considerate of one's wife calls for vigilance,
especially in areas of speech. We tend to be careless
with what we say, and yet a harsh word can inflict
wounds that never heal. In general human relationships,
the Torah prohibits אונאת דברים, causing pain with words,
on which the *Sefer HaChinnuch* elaborates, "One must
not say anything that will pain or anguish someone,
and leave him helpless." Now if this is the case in
regard to strangers, imagine how much more sensitive
the Torah expects one to be towards his wife. A harsh
word, a demeaning expression, an insulting remark, any
of these can severely strain a marriage. A derogatory
name hurled out in anger can inflict a wound that
continues to fester long after the reasons for the
argument are forgotten.

The sensitivity of marital harmony is evident in
God's modification of Sarah's remarks about her
husband, Avraham, when He had questioned them.
Sarah had laughed when she heard that she was to bear
a son, and said, "How is it possible that I, in my
advanced stage in life, should have a son — *and my
husband is old?*" In reporting her comment to Avraham,
God altered the last phrase, to refer to Sarah's own age
instead (*Beraishis* 19:13-14). What harm would there
have been if God had quoted her accurately? Avraham
was 99 years old, had reached an extremely high
spiritual level, and had even prayed for the outward
signs of old age. It would thus seem absurd for
Avraham to be concerned about such petty matters as
his alleged lack of youthfulness.

Yet God deemed it important to circumvent the
issue: Sarah's words were true, they reflected a

fulfillment of Avraham's own prayer, and had they been uttered by anyone else, it is not likely that Avraham would have taken offense at them. But when two lives become so intertwined and mutually dependent as do the lives of a husband and wife, then their relationship is so sensitive that a word or expression uttered in innocence can cause deep hurt and actually threaten *shalom bayis.*

It is a pity that courtship — with its carefully honed phrases, so meticulously worded to avoid misunderstanding — comes to an abrupt end with marriage.

Just as an unpleasant word can have devastating effects on a marriage, a kind word can do wonders to solidify a marriage.

A *talmid* of HaGaon Rav Aaron Kotler, *z.tz.l.*, recalls once driving the *rosh yeshiva* to Lakewood from his home in Boro Park. Reb Aaron was already seated in the car when he suddenly excused himself and asked the driver if he would mind waiting a moment while he took care of something in his house. The *talmid* followed the *rosh yeshiva* up to his third floor apartment to be of assistance if necessary. They entered the apartment, and Reb Aaron went to his *rebbetzin*, wished her, "*A gutten tag*," turned around and left. In his haste, it seems, he had left the house without bidding her good-bye.... The *talmid* says that to this day he remembers the glow of pleasure that lit up the *rebbetzin*'s face because of this simple gesture.

### THE BEST, FROM THE WORST

At times it can be difficult to be appreciative and considerate, when it seems to the husband that the wife is all wrong, impossible to deal with, and so on. The rabbis of the Talmud, however, demonstrated for us how to find the resources for appreciation under all circumstances.

Rav Chiya's wife was known to cause him great anguish throughout their married life. Yet, whenever Rav Chiya saw an item that he thought she might appreciate, he purchased it for her as a gift. Rav Chiya's nephew, Rav, noticed this and asked his uncle why he went out of his way to treat her so graciously when all he received from her was abuse. Rav Chiya replied that "the fact that she raises our children and saves me from sin is sufficient cause for gratitude. The little aggravation she gives me is insignificant in comparison to the tremendous benefits she bestows upon me."

By contrast, *Adam HaRishon* is described as an ingrate by *Chazal* (the rabbis of the Talmud) for blaming his wife for having fed him the forbidden fruit ("The woman that You gave me — she offered me the fruit...," as if the fault lies with the "*Shadchan*"). He had forgotten how he had searched among all the creatures of the world for a mate, to no avail, and he had forgotten how, when God put him to sleep and created Chava and brought her to him, his joy knew no bounds, and he exclaimed ecstatically, "This time, a bone from my bones, flesh from my flesh — this shall be called 'woman'!" The joy was forgotten in the rush of incrimination.

So, too, in many a marriage, when minor differences arise, one partner tends to magnify the problem and fault the spouse for the problem. In a moment of anger, he can deeply hurt the very person to whom he owes so much, overlooking all of the joy and happiness his spouse has brought him over the years. This is the ultimate in ingratitude.

## THE INEVITABLE DIFFERENCES

Since it is impossible for two people living together to agree on absolutely everything, it would be wise to anticipate the inevitable differences that are bound to arise. Is there any preferred way to iron out these differences so as not to strain their relationship?

A recently married young man sought my advice regarding a problem that had arisen in his marriage — a problem that to me seemed to be very insignificant. When I asked him why he thought it necessary to make an issue over such an unimportant thing, he replied, "That's not the idea. Sure, I can give in on this matter. But I'm afraid that if I do, she'll dominate our marriage." I explained to him that his basic premise was foolish. Any relationship is a two-way street. If he would yield on this issue, he would build up credit with his wife, and she, in turn, would be more than willing to please him on other issues that may be far more important to him. And it is not a matter of keeping score on major points but one of dividing areas of responsibility and yielding whenever it is a matter outside of the individual's purview.

## THE DIVISION

How do husband and wife divide their areas of responsibility? *Chazal* have given us a practical suggestion: מילי דעלמא, mundane matters, such as those that pertain to managing the house, are primarily the woman's domain. מילי דשמיא, spiritual matters, should generally be under the husband's jurisdiction.

The husband should not concern himself excessively with the cooking nor become overly involved with decorating the house. He can offer his opinion and should show interest and express appreciation in these areas and — to be sure — offer his help when it is needed. But he should bow to his wife's decision whenever there is a difference in their views.

By the same token, the husband should make the final decision in matters such as selecting the yeshiva for their children, their butcher (in terms of *kashrus*), and the customs they will observe. He should surely discuss the matter with her and take her opinions into account, but he must carry the burden of deciding. He is the *posaik acharon*, the final authority. When the husband does not have a strong religious background, the couple should consult a *rav* and follow his guidance.

### THE SAVING GRACE

The author of *Torah Temima* (in his historical work, *Mekor Baruch*) relates a story that involved his uncle, the *Netziv* — Rabbi Naftoli Tzvi Yehuda Berlin. A distinguished and charitable businessman, who had at one time been recognized as a *lamdan*, came to the *Netziv* to discuss a personal problem. While he was universally respected as a prominent citizen of his community and made an excellent livelihood, no sooner would he cross the threshold of his house, but he became a nonentity. His wife completely dominated the household and ignored him, except to berate him. He felt like a stranger in his own home, which was a source of endless anguish to him.

The *Netziv* asked him if he set aside specific times during the day for Torah study. The man replied that he had become so involved in his business that he did not have the time to establish a *seder*. The *Netziv* stated emphatically, "You must resolve to establish a regular *seder* for a few hours every day — no matter how busy you might be. You must immerse yourself in your Talmudic studies and make it an integral, inviolable part of your life. If you heed my advice, I can assure you that your situation will improve greatly."

The *Mekor Baruch* relates that when he subsequently met his cousin, Rabbi Chaim Berlin, the son of the *Netziv*, he asked him about how this incident was resolved. Reb Chaim replied, "I am familiar with the entire story, and I know the merchant personally. As a matter of fact, whenever his business brings him to Moscow, he stops by to tell me how grateful he is to my father for his wonderful advice. His entire home life has changed ever since he began setting aside time for intensive Torah study. His wife now respects him and treats him with the utmost deference."

The advice of the *Netziv* was not some magical formula, but rather a logical suggestion. Once the woman saw that her husband had reordered his priorities and that Torah had assumed a place of prominence in his life, she realized that she was married to a truly respectable individual and accorded him the honor such a person is entitled to.

## THE "FRUMKEIT" FACTOR

*Shalom bayis* can sometimes be upset because the husband, for instance, is dismayed with his wife's carelessness in matters pertaining to *kashrus* — she accidentally mixes meat and dairy dishes, and *she'ailos* result. So he accuses her of lacking religious vigilance, and he complains to their rabbi. Often there is no basis for the *she'aila* other than the husband's ignorance of *halacha*. At other times, the *she'aila* is with good cause — but this is still no reason for anger. After all, *she'ailos* only arise among Torah-observant people. The mere fact that she presents the *she'aila* to her husband testifies to her high standards of religious concern. The non-observant never bother to ask.

Then, arguments arise when one partner has a *minhag* (custom) or *chumra* (stringent practice) that the other does not share, and the first refuses to yield on it. As worthy as the practice may be, it surely does not measure up to the *shalom bayis* that is being sacrificed in its behalf. If only both parties would consider this, they would put aside their difficulties and spare themselves much anguish.

If the point of contention is a matter of *halacha*, then instead of yielding on it because of *shalom bayis* considerations, one must seek guidance from a *rav*. Generally, whether dealing with *halacha, minhag,* or *chumra* — one would be wise to consult a *rav* to determine what is the proper thing to do.

STRIFE INSURANCE

As much as one should endeavor to avoid strife, all the more so must one try to prevent it in advance. This is best done by imbuing young people with a sensitivity for harmony in interpersonal affairs, but especially as it relates to *shalom bayis*. The burden of prevention is shared by many people. Parents must always bear in mind that they serve as models to their children, and the way they express mutual respect or sharp differences to one another makes its impression on their children, even when they are small.

Teachers and *rebbe'im* can also play an important role in "strife prevention" by extending friendship to their students, earning their trust, and maintaining contact with them after they have left school, by making them feel that their doors are always open to them should the need arise. In this way, when marital problems do threaten, the former student will feel free to return and discuss them with the teacher/*rebbe*, before they mushroom into serious breaches of *shalom bayis*. Finally, and most important, every individual must increase his awareness that his purpose in life is to increase *kavod Shamayim* — to enhance God's glory in the world by leading a Torah life and raising a good family, דור ישרים יבורך. When one leads a life consistent with Torah, then all interpersonal dealings should conform with the ideal of "ways of pleasantness"; all the more so should this be the case in regard to all that passes between husband and wife.

# CHAPTER ONE

# Who Needs Preparation for Marriage?

"Dovid, if you don't start looking now for a new *chavrusa*, you will never be ready for the new *zman*!"

"You'd better study your *chumash* more often, Esty, if you're serious about graduating seminary this year!"

These are familiar sounds in many Torah homes. Preparation for all levels of Torah study is taken seriously by most of your parents. Your parents are not professional educators, only *shomrai mitzvos*, following the teachings of the *Gemara* (Talmud), that preparing a child (and providing) for Torah study is a major parental responsibility (*Kiddushin* 29a).

The *Gemara* also includes preparation for other of life's necessities, such as having a trade and knowing how to swim, in this list of parental responsibilities. With equal zeal, then, your parents also plan for your vocational training or means of providing a livelihood. Finding the proper *shidduch*, the *Gemara* explains, is another top priority.

Unfortunately, the preparation often stops there. Today, marriage (and parenthood) are taken too much for granted. At 19, 20 — or 22, 23 — you are automatically considered ready for marriage, without any preparation.

To be a proper spouse and a proper parent are probably the greatest challenges you will ever face, and yet you are expected to face these challenges with hardly any specific preparation.

If your parents have not fulfilled their responsibilities of preparing you for life's necessities, are you totally absolved? If you have not succeeded in your Torah studies, is it all your parents' fault? If you enter adulthood with no vocational skills, can you only blame your parents? And if your parents have not taught you how to swim, can you never find someone else to teach you?

Even in the best circumstances, parents can never be expected to complete the job of preparing you for life. They can only hope to get you started on the right foot. But whether or not they helped you get started, the buck stops at your doorstep. So if you received inadequate swimming lessons, why should you allow yourself to flounder in the sea of family life? And even if you received excellent lessons, can your preparation for family life ever be "completed"?

It is your life and your marriage which will stand or fall depending upon what you bring to it. Even though you may already be engaged now, or even married, it is never too late to prepare today for a better tomorrow.

No, our *bubbies* and *zaidies* (grandparents) never had any preparation for marriage beyond what they saw at home. But, then again, their generation also did not witness the epidemic of divorces plaguing our community today.

Needless to say, many complex factors contribute to the tragic breakdown of today's young families. Nevertheless, with proper preparation, at least some of these divorces could have been prevented.

But not every unhappy marriage ends in divorce. Far more unsuccessful marriages continue, providing years of suffering, devoid of *shalom bayis*. The young people who entered these marriages also would have benefited from additional preparation before marriage.

Of course, not every unhappy marriage can be attributed to inadequate preparation. But most can. And certainly *all* marriages would be enhanced by additional attention to preparation beforehand. So the answer to the question "Who needs preparation?" is really, "Everyone."

# CHAPTER TWO

# How to Prepare for Marriage

"O.K., so it is important for me to make sure that I am properly prepared for marriage. But how am I supposed to go about preparing myself?"

The best way to prepare yourself for marriage is to discuss all aspects of marriage and family life with your parents and *mechanchim*. Raise your questions and share your concerns with them, now. Sometimes, even concerns which don't seem to be related to marriage could have an impact on your future married life. Therefore, one of the best ways to begin preparing for marriage is to develop and maintain open lines of communication with your parents and *mechanchim*.

## The Role of Parents

In order to illustrate the need for you to maintain open communication with your parents, a brief case history will be presented. It should be stressed at the outset that although the cases cited in this book are drawn from my clinical practice, all identifying information has been thoroughly disguised in order to protect the confidentiality of the individuals involved. In fact, any similarities between these cases and actual situations you are familiar with should be attributed only to the widespread nature of these problems.

**Rivka** was always a good student and her parents heard only praises from her teachers. Although quiet, she kept up with a small circle of close friends all during her elementary-school years.

Shortly after beginning high school, however, Rivka seemed to become even more quiet than before. Her contacts with friends decreased and the occasional smile was now seldom seen on her face.

Rivka's parents attributed her seriousness to the increased academic demands of high school. "Surely by next year," they reasoned, "Rivka will outgrow this."

By her senior year, Rivka had no friends, went out of the house only for errands and school, and spent most of her time in her room. Her parents received positive reports of Rivka's academic progress, and they continued to assume that she would "outgrow" her withdrawn nature. Student teaching in seminary, they concluded, would help to "bring her out."

Two years later, the picture remained the same. Many of Rivka's classmates were becoming engaged. Her parents speculated that she was envious of the other girls, yearning for her own *chassan*. They inquired about *shidduchim* and, after she had several meetings with Chaim, a well-recommended *talmid* from a high-caliber yeshiva, they encouraged Rivka to accept his marriage proposal.

Before the end of her first year of marriage, Rivka became so upset with marital problems that she wanted to leave Chaim and move back to her parents' home. Both sets of parents encouraged the couple to consult a *rav*, who eventually referred them for professional help.

 **Chaim** refused to meet with the professional and preferred to speak with another *rav*. Two years later, after many frustrated efforts to resolve the marital conflicts, Rivka and Chaim were divorced. Chaim remained in the couple's apartment and Rivka returned to her parents' home with her baby.

Rivka's parents knew of the first *rav*'s efforts to refer Rivka and Chaim for professional help, so they encouraged her to meet with the family counselor.

Chaim was never seen by the counselor. From Rivka's reports of his behavior, however, it was clear that he also brought his own "*peckeleh*" of emotional difficulties to the marriage.

In time, with professional help, Rivka unraveled the mysteries of her own feelings. She was able to trace her emotional problems back, as you have undoubtedly already done, to well before her marriage, to her high-school days. A detailed record of the treatment process is not relevant here. Suffice it to say that Rivka has since gotten a job, established her own home, and has begun to build meaningful and satisfying friendships.

The crucial aspect of this case was the relationship between Rivka and her parents. Although they were deeply concerned and loving parents, they felt more comfortable consulting Rivka's teachers and a *rav* than consulting Rivka herself. It was never easy for them to sit down and talk with any of their four children. Rivka, however, was the hardest to talk with because she was the most withdrawn. As a result, she was the first to be overlooked by her parents.

No one can say just what would have happened if Rivka's parents had made greater efforts to really get to know her. It is, of course, quite possible that their initiatives might have been rebuffed by Rivka anyway. In other words, just because her parents would have tried to learn from Rivka what was bothering her does not mean that she would have been able to tell them. Nevertheless, greater direct involvement by Rivka's parents could have resulted, at the very least, in seeking professional help while she was still in high school. Had she done so, it is very possible that her trip to the *chuppa* (wedding canopy) would have been only "one way."

But parent-child communication works in both directions. Just as Rivka's parents should have made greater efforts to understand her, she also should have made greater efforts to share her concerns with them. Had she done so, perhaps her parents could have helped her resolve the difficulty. But even if they could not, they would have appreciated the seriousness of Rivka's problems and then acted accordingly.

Case illustrations are as dangerous as they are helpful. Defensive, frightened young people can read Rivka's story and respond smugly, "Oh, that doesn't apply to *me!*" Rivka's story, however, is unfortunately all too common. Many yeshiva and Bais Yaakov children grow up without ever really being able to communicate freely with their parents. And when this is the case, small problems in childhood can grow into big problems in marriage, unnecessarily. But even when there are no problems in childhood, poor parent-child communication can deprive you of the valuable guidance, advice and experience of your parents which could help you as you prepare for your own marriage.

## The Role of Educators

The parent-child relationship is only one source of marriage guidance which you may not be exploiting fully. The *rebbe-talmid* relationship is another potential source of marriage guidance. In order to take full advantage of this opportunity, you will have to reach out to your *mechanchim* with your questions.

Of course, just as with your parents, you do not carry the full responsibility for maintaining open lines of communication. Your *mechanchim* must do their part to provide you with ample opportunities to air your concerns about dating, courtship and marriage.

Several Torah institutions have taken the initiative in providing their students with a broader-based preparation for marriage. Hopefully, their pioneering efforts will pave the way for others to follow.

The Be'er Yaakov Yeshiva, in Eretz Yisrael, offered a series of *vaadim* (small group conferences) with the now former *mashgiach ruchani*, Rabbi Shlomo Wolbe, on topics of marital life. In these *vaadim*, Rabbi Wolbe discussed such topics as the emotional needs of a wife and the husband's responsibility to meet them, the qualitative differences between the close relationship of a *bachur* (young man) and his *chavrusa* (study partner) and the husband-wife relationship; the meaning to a wife of the appearance of the home; the emotional and spiritual differentiation between man and woman, and how this can lead to a harmonious complementarity or, *chas v'shalom* (Heaven forbid), to frustrating conflict.

Rabbi Wolbe has printed a booklet on these discussions which, due to the specific legacy of his late father-in-law, Rabbi Avrohom Grodzensky, *z.tz.l.*, is not available to the public.

Rabbi Wolbe has written a second booklet, in consultation with Rebbetzin Jacobson of Yerushalayim, designed for young women, which *is* available to the general public. This booklet, together with a foreword written by Rabbi Yehuda Meisels, has been published by the Beth Jacob Sara Schenirer High School and Teachers Seminary in Brooklyn, New York.

In the second booklet, Rabbi Wolbe discusses such topics as the impact of life in a yeshiva dormitory on a *bachur*, and the many changes needed for him to adjust to married life; the importance of patience and tolerance from both *chassan* and *kalla* during the first year of marriage;

and the necessity of avoiding the all-too-common hazard of sharing private, husband-wife matters with others — friends or relatives.

One particular girls' school in the New York area sponsored voluntary marriage-oriented discussion groups for the senior class, led by a married professional who adheres to the same Torah values held by the yeshiva. In these discussions, the girls had the opportunity to share their expectations for and apprehensions of courtship and marriage, as well as to clarify many of their misconceptions.

Mrs. Shulamis Rogoff, a former consultant who led that school's discussion groups, remarked, "Some of the girls were very upset by the current attitudes associated with dating and *shidduchim*." Mrs. Rogoff found that these groups provided the girls with an opportunity to share their concerns openly and learn that they were not alone, out-of-step or "crazy."

The girls spoke for themselves:

"When a *shidduch* will be *red* (spoken) to me, I know that means that I will be looked over by so many other people, that it makes me sick. Sometimes, I feel that I'd rather not go out than have to face this 'marriage market' ordeal!"

"Somehow, I find it all so confusing. For eighteen years it gets drummed into my head that I'm not supposed to talk to, look at, or even think about boys. Then, all of a sudden, literally overnight, I'm supposed to be able not only to go out with boys but also to feel relaxed on the date!"

"I'd like to know why all decisions about marriage are supposed to be made by the fourth or fifth date. Just knowing that I would have that kind of deadline would make me too nervous to evaluate a situation clearly!"

Ultimately these discussions helped the girls to gain a

clearer understanding of marriage in general and themselves in particular, all from a Torah perspective and in a Torah environment. These discussions also helped the girls to appreciate the superiority of our system of *shidduchim* and dating over that of the secular world.

Mrs. Rogoff pointed out that another one of the goals of these sessions was to help the girls clarify what it was that they really wanted in a *shidduch*. For example, she talked with the girls about where they should place the relationship factor on their list of priorities.

"Even though the girls didn't believe me," she concluded, "I often reminded them that boys are often worried about exactly the same issues."

The examples cited above are, unfortunately, exceptions rather than the rule. Nevertheless, more and more of these kinds of opportunities are being provided by yeshivos and seminaries to help prepare their *talmidim* and *talmidos* for marriage.

One of the reasons that more opportunities are not provided is that *mechanchim* are not convinced that there is sufficient interest. *Mechanchim* all agree that more preparation for marriage is needed today. But some believe that if *vaadim*, discussion groups, or *schmuesim* (lectures) are offered, they will not be well attended. So one practical step you can take is to remove any doubt at your own yeshiva or seminary. If discussion groups are available, you should take full advantage of this valuable opportunity. And if they are not available, let your *mechanchim* know that you would be interested in participating if such opportunities could be organized.

It is highly doubtful whether marriage-oriented discussion groups would have helped Rivka. If such a group had been available to her, she might have chosen not to attend. Even if she did attend, she would have been quite passive and uninvolved. Her emotional problems were too deeply rooted at home. In *other* cases, however, in spite of problems originating in the family, a yeshiva or seminary can play a vital role in preparing young people for marriage.

The next case illustrates when a class or discussion group might have helped. Of course, no one can say for sure just what impact group sessions would have had. Nevertheless, the chances of a more positive outcome would have been greatly increased.

 **Reuven** came from what could be described as a "middle-of-the-road" Orthodox family. Although his father did not have an extensive yeshiva background, Reuven's parents did not object to his decision to continue his full-time yeshiva studies after high school. While they did question him about his future vocational plans and prospects, they never pressured him to leave the yeshiva.

At twenty-six, Reuven was not the oldest *bachur* in the yeshiva, but all of his close friends were already married. Even though his parents did not pressure him to get married, Reuven still felt overwhelmed by the subtle social pressure of his peers.

Reuven had always been a somewhat tense young man. This was due, in part, to the marital conflict between his parents, which he observed at home. Reuven adapted to the unpleasant family environment by ignoring it to the best of his ability. When he couldn't ignore it, he planned elaborate avoidance maneuvers. Reuven learned to use a similar approach in dealing with all of his anxieties. They never went away, nor did his parents' marital conflict disappear, but at least he was able to live with them.

When Reuven's *chavrusa*, two years his junior, became engaged, Reuven panicked. He had often felt self-conscious, but now he felt even more so. He became tormented by his single status and felt compelled to get married.

Reuven's apprehensions were not unusual, but his way

of dealing with them had some very unfortunate consequences.

What were Reuven's worries? First of all, he was afraid that he would make an improper mate selection and thereby condemn himself to repeat his parents' turmoil. In addition, since many of his parents' arguments focused on financial matters, Reuven feared poverty. With no realistic vocational plans, Reuven hesitated taking on the financial responsibility of marriage. Finally, he knew that he had coped with unpleasant feelings in the past by ignoring them and he had handled anxiety-provoking situations by strategically planning to avoid them. This time, however, Reuven realized that denial and avoidance just weren't going to work.

Even while out on a date, Reuven was plagued with these thoughts and was painfully aware of how inadequate his old adaptations were to this new situation. "How absurd!" he thought to himself. "Here I am, going out and at the same time I'm hoping that nothing comes of it!"

Characteristically, he did not discuss his fears with any friends although he was most eager to do so. But even Reuven couldn't completely suppress his fears of marriage by the time he turned twenty-six.

He consulted the *mashgiach* of his yeshiva. He was so self-conscious, however, that he could not be completely open, and he failed to present his problem in its fullest proportions. He posed the problem in vague financial terms and, as a result, received an inadequate response. How could the *mashgiach* know what was really troubling Reuven? Certainly he could not have been expected to read Reuven's mind!

Reuven finally did become engaged — to Chaya, a seminary graduate now working as a secretary. When thinking of his vocational plans, he tried, unsuccessfully, to satisfy himself with vague generalities and abstract prospects. Every time he thought about it, he became more and more anxious. In addition, the slightest, normal disagreement with Chaya aggravated his fears of repeating his parents' mistakes. Furthermore, the multitude of new situations with Chaya, future in-laws, wedding plans, and so on, challenged his avoidance strategies. He had difficulty learning as his uncertainties snowballed. He became depressed, feared it was noticeable and tried desperately to hide this, too.

Reuven's marriage to Chaya lasted an agonizing five months.

Although Chaya certainly could have been much more supportive of Reuven, his apprehensions and anxieties clearly planted the seeds for this divorce. While many of Reuven's worries originated at home, questions about financial responsibilities in marriage, about coping with the future, about the inevitable strains in the husband-wife relationship and about avoiding the pitfalls of one's parents are most common. Many young men and women share similar, even identical concerns. Some of them diffuse the time bomb of these concerns with hours of heart-to-heart talks with friends, relatives, and *rabbanim*. A large number of young men and women, however — similar to Reuven — try to cope with these valid questions by ignoring them or suppressing them. In spite of such efforts, these questions often reappear later, in much more frightening and unmanageable dimensions.

Reuven was convinced that his *mashgiach* would have ridiculed him, had he shared his fears openly. That is most doubtful. Nevertheless, if a marriage-oriented discussion group or *vaad* had been available to him, it is likely that Reuven would have attended. Even if he wouldn't have "opened up" there, hearing the similar concerns of others might have had a positive, cathartic effect in calming his tensions.

Shortly after his divorce, Reuven sought help at a local vocational guidance service. The perceptive counselor referred Reuven to a psychotherapist for individual counseling. This counseling, in part, addressed issues of concern for Reuven which could have been effectively handled in a premarital discussion group. Had this been the case, Reuven would have been much better prepared for marriage and, in all probability, his marriage to Chaya would have been more successful.

## Conclusion

There are no simple answers to difficult questions. Even if you have developed open lines of communication with your parents and *mechanchim*, your future *shalom bayis* is not guaranteed. Nevertheless, your chances of achieving *shalom bayis* will be greatly increased if you have taken full advantage of the guidance offered by your parents and *mechanchim*.

You may, however, feel like the *she'aino yodai'a lishol*, the fourth son mentioned in the *Haggada* who "knows not what to ask." In the chapters which follow, some of the most commonly asked questions about dating and marriage are presented together with some answers. No effort has been made to include all possible questions, so don't be disappointed if all of *your* questions are not addressed. Those which have been included, however, are all questions which you *should* be thinking about and which, hopefully, you will be discussing not only with your friends, but with your parents and *mechanchim* as well.

# CHAPTER THREE

# Great Expectations: What Marriage Is and Is Not

## What Marriage Is

Marriage is a *nissayon* — not in the sense of being an "ordeal" but as a "test." As one of life's greatest opportunities, marriage is a test as to how well we will take advantage of what it offers.

The opportunities, of course, are not unlimited. One's choice of spouse is certainly a factor in what can be achieved. Generally, though, those who approach marriage as an opportunity invest more in it than those who view marriage as a solution.

Marriage can also be understood as a partnership in which both spouses must try to contribute 90% in order to enjoy an equal share of the benefits. To paraphrase the late President John F. Kennedy, "Ask not what your spouse can do for you, but rather what you can do for your spouse!"

Finally, marriage can be compared to a plant. In order to grow properly, a number of necessary conditions must be met. The roots must be firmly grounded in a soil rich in nutrients. There must be ample supplies of air and sunlight. Last, but not least, the plant must be watered moderately, on a regular basis. Both excessive watering and insufficient watering can easily kill any plant.

How does this apply to marriage? A successful marriage is one in which the roots are firmly grounded in Torah values. There must be ample supplies of appreciation and affection. Last, but not least, each spouse must devote at least moderate attention to the other spouse *on a regular basis.*

To be sure, there is much more to say, and volumes have been written about marriage from the Torah perspective. Although a complete review of Torah thoughts on marriage is far beyond the scope of this book, an excellent introduction to *da'as Torah* concerning marriage is the essay of HaRav Avrohom Pam, *shlita*, "The Jewish Home: Mainstay of Our People," (the Introductory Essay of this book). And no one should even consider overlooking the Rambam, *Sefer Nashim, Hilchos Ishus,* chapters 12 through 15.

## What Marriage Is Not

Just as you need to know what marriage is, you also need to know what it is not. Many young people have a thoroughly distorted view of marriage, and their expectations are totally unrealistic. If you get married without first correcting these misconceptions, you run the risk of facing deep disappointment or, worse, marital conflict and discord.

The misconceptions which follow may strike someone who is happily married for many years as unusual or unbelievable. To many of you, however, they may sound all too familiar.

**"MARRIAGE IS A SOLUTION FOR LONELINESS, DEPRESSION AND FEELINGS OF INFERIORITY."**

Certainly marriage does provide companionship, encouragement and feelings of being important to someone else. It was clearly in the design of Creation for people to have certain needs fulfilled through marriage, as the Torah states: "It is not good for Man to be alone" (*Beraishis* 2:18). A single person with many friends, for example, still experiences a void which can be filled only through marriage. This is normal and appropriate. Nevertheless, marriage cannot provide a cure for deep-seated emotional problems or social handicaps. If someone is beset with so many emotional difficulties that he or she has failed to make friends, then the complex challenges of married life will probably only add another failure to the long list of earlier ones.

Should depressed or lonely people not get married? Of course they should. But these young people should seek out the guidance and advice of their parents, *rebbe'im*, mentors or anyone else equipped to help them work toward overcoming these hurdles *before* taking on the challenges of marriage. They should not expect marriage to solve their problems.

One respected *ben Torah*, who is now happily married to his second wife, confided to me, "When I was eighteen years old, I and all of my friends in yeshiva honestly believed that whatever problems we had would somehow disappear after we would stand under the *chuppa*. To tell you the truth, if I had not been such a hothead and hadn't run off to a *rav* for a *get* (divorce) after only two weeks, my first marriage might have been saved."

This young man was not a patient of mine, nor did he ever receive any form of mental health service. He was simply sharing his personal experience with me in the hope that I pass it on and help others avoid the same mistakes.

Another one who fell into the trap of unrealistic expectations was Tzippy. She shared the same misconceptions as the *ben Torah* quoted above.

 **Tzippy** always had friends and was considered popular throughout high school. She did well academically and was involved in *chessed* and *kiruv* work. Unlike Rivka (chapter 2), Tzippy had an open, close relationship with both of her parents. In spite of all her many academic and social achievements, however, Tzippy always felt slightly inadequate. For example, she always felt inferior to her friends, and sometimes she even questioned whether or not they *really* liked her. Tzippy never felt her grades were high enough, and she seldom took pride in her volunteer work. In fact, if anyone ever offered Tzippy approval or a compliment, she would chalk it off to either bad judgment or insincere flattery.

After graduating seminary, when Tzippy began to anticipate marriage, she looked forward to the increased security and self-confidence that she was certain marriage would bring. When she finally married Moshe, Tzippy was absolutely thrilled. He came from such a fine background and had so many good qualities that she truly believed she was not worthy of such a *shidduch*.

Shortly after the wedding Tzippy's doubts grew into fears. "Does Moshe really need me as much as I need him?" she began to wonder. As a result, she started to insist that he consult and collaborate with her on every decision including those he had to make at work. She didn't really want to infantalize Moshe, but she did want him to need her as much as she needed him.

Moshe resented what he saw as Tzippy's interference. He felt she was trying to control him and rob him of his autonomy. Moshe responded by cutting off Tzippy abruptly and, at times, even rudely. He would then refuse to talk.

When Tzippy would be cut off this way, she felt totally rejected. This played into her feelings of inadequacy and inferiority. She would feel insecure and frightened. As a result, Tzippy would lash out at Moshe whenever he cut her off, and enormous blow-ups would ensue.

Tzippy and Moshe's marital conflict had two primary causes. Moshe was too abrupt, at times, certainly. But

Tzippy's insecurity about herself pushed her to behave in a provocative way toward Moshe. She always felt insecure about herself, even before marriage. But when her self-confidence problems did not disappear after marriage, as she had expected, her disappointment and anxiety only increased.

This is not to imply that Tzippy should have avoided marriage. But she should not have fooled herself into believing that her feelings of inadequacy and inferiority would be miraculously erased by marriage. Such unrealistic expectations were initially very soothing to Tzippy, but they eventually led to disappointment and resentment.

Ideally, Tzippy should have sought more appropriate solutions to her self-esteem problems, *before* getting married. She might have consulted with one of her *mechanchim*, for example, in search of ways to overcome her nagging self-doubts. There are many methods which can successfully help someone to overcome this problem. Getting married, however, is *not* one of them.

### "MARRIAGE IS A SOLUTION FOR IMMATURITY AND IRRESPONSIBILITY."

Anyone who has enjoyed the relative independence of being single can certainly find the increased responsibilities of marriage a maturing experience. Suddenly, money, time and other resources need to be budgeted more carefully. Another person's needs and desires must be taken into account in a new and more intense fashion than ever before.

These facts of married life do help young people mature as they grow into new responsibilities and adjust to them. But marriage itself can never create maturity, *yaish me'ayin* (ex nihilo), imbuing a person with a sense of responsibility where none existed before.

Take, for example, the common area of going to bed and getting up on time. Single people are notorious for keeping late hours — probably a time-honored custom for many generations. The demands of married life often force people into a more practical and responsible schedule. Instead of going to bed at 1:30 A.M. and getting up at 8:00 A.M., a young married person may retire at 11:30 P.M. and arise before 7:00 A.M.

If, on the other hand, someone's daily routine is so severely impaired that he or she has no schedule whatsoever, marriage per se will not be the answer.

 **Yehudah** was one of the older *bachurim* in the yeshiva and was seen by many to fit into a category of his own. He never managed to hold onto a *chavrusa* for any significant length of time. During most of the day he learned alone, with the exception of the 45-minute *Mishna Brura seder* (period), when Yehudah learned with the *rosh yeshiva*'s son.

Aside from all of his idiosyncrasies, the most prominent feature of Yehudah's personality was his daily routine. He would retire in the evening anytime between 9 P.M. and 4 A.M., although usually it was closer to 4 A.M. The only consistent feature of his schedule was that he *never* got up on time to attend morning *minyan*. In fact, there were many days when he even missed breakfast in the yeshiva because he got up so late.

Some friends were very involved with Yehudah and agreed with him that by getting married he would be forced into more responsible behavior. Yehudah was, of course, in serious trouble. But to someone like Yehudah, marriage can mean even greater trouble.

Unfortunately, you and your friends are not the only ones who may mistakenly assume that marriage will solve chronic problems of immaturity and irresponsibility. Your parents may also share this misconception.

**Sarah** is an attractive twenty-one-year-old girl from a deeply religious family. Sarah does not work or attend any educational programs. She lost her last three jobs due to lateness, low productivity and absenteeism. According to Sarah's mother, however, "Sarah is such a lovely girl. She is so *aiydle* [refined] and *frum*. All she needs now is to find the right *shidduch*. I'm sure that once she has her own home, she will straighten out."

The sad fact is that if Sarah does not "straighten out" *before* she gets married, the prospects for her marriage are quite bleak. She will inevitably approach her household responsibilities in the same indifferent, immature and haphazard fashion in which she approached her responsibilities at home, school and work. Since obviously her parents cannot offer Sarah proper guidance, they should direct her to someone else who can. As long as Sarah's parents expect marriage to have a therapeutic impact on their daughter, she stands a good chance of adding to the already unacceptable statistics of divorce.

As my *chavrusa* in our yeshiva days summed it up (we were both single at the time), "I'm fully aware that getting married will not solve any of my problems. But I'm just getting to the point in life where I'm tired of my old problems and I'm ready for new ones!"

No one can expect to know all about marriage before getting married. And few of us are ready to make the same investment as Yaakov Avinu who spent fourteen years in the yeshiva of Shem V'Aiver preparing for his marriage (see Rashi's commentary on *Beraishis* 28:11). So once you have debunked your misconceptions about marriage and once you have adopted a more realistic outlook, you are ready to address the next questions of dating and courtship.

# CHAPTER FOUR

# Guidelines for Dating and Courtship

Even those of you who might try to delude yourselves into thinking that you know all about marriage (i.e., "What's there to know?"), will have to admit that you could use guidance in the area of dating.

The four questions asked most often regarding dating are: When to start? What to look for? How much to reveal? and How long to date the same person before deciding on marriage? Most likely, you have already discussed at least one of these questions with your friends. Nevertheless, you would do well to discuss all four with your parents and *rebbe'im.*

## When to Start Dating?

Most young people tend to be well attuned to their own internal timetable and are the best judges of when they are "ready." Others do need some assistance. As a general guideline, you would do well to examine your expectations of marriage. If they are out of line with a realistic conception of marriage (see chapter 3), then you should consider yourself "not ready."

But can someone feel "not ready" when in fact he or she may not only be "ready" but "overdue"? In other words, can someone be overly cautious about waiting? The answer is a resounding "Yes!" If so, how can those in doubt accurately assess their own readiness for marriage?

Questions of this nature are too individualized to be handled in groups or through published guidelines and can only be adequately addressed in one-to-one discussions. Group sessions can be very beneficial, however, by introducing young people to *rabbanim* to whom they can turn for private conferences on this and other subjects.

When you do consult your *rebbe'im* on the question of when to start going out, bear in mind that there is considerable difference of opinion among *rebbe'im* on this subject. Of course, this does not mean that you should "shop around" for the advice that pleases you. To do that would be self-defeating. Rather, you should discuss the subject with *rebbe'im* who know you *personally* and who can take your individual needs, strengths and weaknesses into account. Some *rebbe'im*, for example, could have strong opinions which they may apply across the board. While I certainly do not question these opinions or the judgment of the *rebbe'im* who hold them, you should feel free to seek a "second opinion" if you suspect that your individual needs are being overlooked.

 **Yosef,** a twenty-one-year-old *bachur*, was learning in an out-of-town yeshiva. He was completing his preparation for a career in *chinnuch* and decided that he was ready to get married (i.e., begin dating).

Yosef discussed this first with his parents who were neither in favor nor opposed. They left this and other major decisions completely up to him. Being the methodical type, Yosef decided to consult with his *rebbe'im* in the yeshiva. He consulted with two.

Both *rebbe'im* strongly discouraged him. They did not cite any personal failing or immaturity in Yosef but rather cited their *shitta* (position) that young men should continue uninterrupted Torah study until they are at least twenty-three or twenty-four before they begin dating.

Although most of the young men in the yeshiva accepted this advice, Yosef was uncomfortable with it. He began to wonder if, perhaps, there were other valid opinions on this subject. Since Yosef came from a Sephardic background, he decided to consult the Sephardic Chief Rabbi of Israel who was in the United States on a visit.

To Yosef's surprise, when he presented his question, the Sephardic Chief Rabbi became irritated and upset. "What? You're twenty-one and not married? What are you waiting for?" the Chief Rabbi demanded. When Yosef explained that he was waiting at the advice of his *rebbe'im*, the Chief Rabbi became indignant. "Why do these Ashkenazi rabbis continue to hold back young men from getting married? Don't they realize that they are restricting the size of the Jewish population?!"

"*Ailu v'ailu divrai Elokim chayim*" (Both these and those are the words of the living God). Yosef never questioned and continued to respect the judgment of his *rebbe'im*. But as a Sephardic Jew, he felt he had made the correct decision to seek a "second opinion" from a Sephardic rabbinic authority. And in keeping with his Sephardic tradition he decided he was ready to accept the Chief Rabbi's advice to begin dating. When he shared this decision with his *rebbe'im* in the yeshiva, he was pleasantly surprised to find them so supportive.

Once the decision to begin dating has been made, the following question is often raised.

## What to Look for?

Perhaps the most succinct, general guideline for selecting a mate was offered by the classical formula of the Talmud: "*baishanim, rachamim, v'gomlai chassadim*" (modest, compassionate, and generously kind). See *Yevamos* 79a and the

Rambam, *Hilchos Isurai Biyah*, chapter 19, paragraph 17, for further elaboration on this guideline. In-depth discussions with your parents and *mechanchim* on the meaning of these three qualities and how to recognize them can provide an excellent starting point for discussing other important factors, such as values and priorities, appearance and personality.

### VALUES AND PRIORITIES

Prospective spouses need to share common values and priorities; what is important to one should be important to the other. While this may seem too obvious to mention, the area of values and priorities can become extremely problematic when the people involved are not fully honest with themselves, or each other.

Suppose, for example, your friends are all adopting a *kollel* life-style after marriage, where the wife works to support the husband's full-time Torah study. Perhaps you do not know what such a life entails, or perhaps you do not truly aspire to that life. Not wanting to stick out from the crowd, however, you express a desire for a *kollel*-type mate.

Any deception — of self or prospective partner — can have tragic consequences. Everyone can appreciate, for example, the need for frankness regarding medical history and family background. In those cases where poor judgment prevailed and overt deception was practiced, the inevitable discovery has often led to marital conflict or divorce. So too in the area of values and priorities, young people need to be honest with themselves and each other in order to prevent heartache and regret later on.

### APPEARANCE

What role should appearance and attractiveness play in selecting a mate? Many young people assume that their teachers and *rabbanim* would advise them not to consider appearance. They even feel they are cheating in some way by looking for an attractive mate. Most *rabbanim*, however, would probably advise that attractiveness *is* important but that it must be kept in perspective. You should never agree to marry someone you find unattractive. At the same time, however, you should not place "good looks" at the top of your list of priorities.

 **Yaakov's** friends and relatives all knew he wanted two things: looks and money. He went out with almost fifty girls until he got married. Everyone thought he got what he wanted and so did Yaakov when he married a very attractive girl from one of the wealthiest Orthodox families in the area. After three years, Yaakov learned the hard way that there is more to marriage than beauty and money. Now divorced, he is looking for a mate who may possess neither beauty nor money, but with whom he will be able to get along.

### PERSONALITY

How much importance should be placed on the relationship factor, that is, on personalities and how the couple get along with each other? Some yeshiva students and seminary graduates tend to pay too little attention to the relationship factor and tend to have little background for making such assessments. Yet the need to evaluate this factor cannot be overemphasized, as a painfully clear clinical observation makes obvious. In all of my experience in working with divorcing couples and divorced individuals, I never met one person who could not recall seeing *before* marriage the very same traits in the ex-spouse that later led to divorce! Before marriage, these people either denied, ignored or overlooked the problems. Of course, many insignificant differences should be overlooked, and others may only become critical later. But if *all* relationship problems are overlooked, serious marital conflict can develop.

Here, as with other fine distinctions, a private consultation with your *rav* or parents would be in place. Once again, there is just too much at stake for you to decide by yourself whether or not to overlook a particular relationship problem.

After you have a clear idea as to what to look for, the next question often surfaces.

## How Much to Reveal?

Just how much personal, medical, or family history needs to be revealed before marriage? Certainly no one should come to the first date with a copy of his medical records. But, on the other hand, no one should try to conceal major chronic illness, as some have tried to do.

The best rule of thumb is as follows: when in doubt, leave it out and then consult a halachic authority, immediately. Enough *teshuvos* (rabbinic responsa) have been published on such questions to emphasize the need for individual, case-specific halachic consultations (see, for example, *Igros Moshe, Orach Chaim*, fourth edition, *siman* 117). Don't decide the matter for yourself. There is simply too much at stake either way.

If you do try to decide for yourself, you might reveal unnecessary information which could result in scuttling a perfectly good *shidduch* needlessly. On the other hand, you also may decide to conceal vital information which could eventually lead to a broken marriage that could have and should have been avoided.

## How Long to Date?

You may wonder: "Does something inside tell me that this person is for me? Do I see stars or hear bells ringing? How do I know?"

One experienced seminary teacher advises his students

this way: "Do you find his company pleasant? Does he possess those character traits and goals in life that you admire? Does he have any habits or attitudes that make you uneasy?" If the answers to the first two questions are positive and the answer to the last is negative, he advises going ahead. He reminds them that Rabbi Samson Raphael Hirsch points out that first the Torah tells us, "Yitzchak brought [Rivka] into the tent of his mother Sarah and he took her…as his wife," and only *after that* "and he loved her" (*Beraishis* 24:67). In a Torah society, true love comes with marriage. When overwhelming infatuation sets in too early, caution is in order.

But how often should you meet each other before you make the final decision?

In spite of all the advice young people inevitably receive, no absolute timetables should be given. Telling single people how long they're supposed to date each other before "deciding" can be destructive, because people's needs vary greatly.

Some single people tend to be more nervous and anxious than others when meeting *shidduchim*, and they may need to see the same person a few more times than their friends do before making a final decision. When pressured to make up their minds, after seeing someone as many times "as everyone else," serious consequences can result.

At the very least, young people who are already quite tense can be made more uneasy. At worst, this pressure can contribute to an incorrect decision. How many good *shidduchim* were broken only because someone insisted, "If you can't decide by the ___th date, then it's probably not for you!" And some unhappy marriages could have been avoided if someone had not coaxed, "If you've already gone out on ___ dates, then you must really be meant for each other!"

Another group of young people run the risk of post-poning a decision almost indefinitely, and they need encouragement to make up their minds. In fact, the longer they see the same *shidduch*, the harder it becomes for them to finally decide. These young people probably spend a year looking for "the right yeshiva" or a month looking for "the right dress." Having always found it difficult to make decisions, they find that deciding about marriage is no exception. To be sure, marriage is a serious matter that demands careful consideration, but even "careful consideration" has limits. Some *young* single people even become *old* single people because they carried "careful consideration" too far.

How do single people know to which group they belong? How do their parents and friends know? If someone says, "I think I need to see him some more before I know for sure," how can you tell if she should be encouraged to take her time or to make up her mind?

Or, to put it more directly, suppose you are hesitant, doubtful or apprehensive about proposing marriage or accepting someone's proposal. This *shidduch* has many pluses which make you reluctant to reject it. On the other hand, you don't feel ready to make a commitment to marriage. How do you know if your concerns are legitimate? How do you know if that "little voice" of caution is the *yaitzer hara* (evil inclination) or the *yaitzer hatov* (good inclination)? How do you know for sure?!

Since these questions are so common and arouse so much stress, tension and anxiety even in people who are otherwise calm and relaxed, the entire next chapter has been devoted to answering them, in depth.

CHAPTER FIVE

# Engagement Anxiety: How Do I Know for Sure?

Many people become anxious, confused and even panicky when faced with a decision about marriage. That is quite common. After all, it is a major decision. But for a few people, the decision of whether or not to marry someone can become completely overwhelming and intolerable.

People in the latter group are often advised not to worry. They are told that their engagement anxiety is normal and it should not be taken too seriously. But is that *always* the best advice? What is "engagement anxiety"? How common is it? If you experience engagement anxiety, how should you deal with it? How should your friends and relatives deal with it? This chapter will address these difficult and most urgent questions.

## What is Engagement Anxiety?

My use of the term "engagement anxiety" is not limited to people who are officially engaged to be married. Engagement anxiety, therefore, includes the doubts, worries, second thoughts and fears associated with any stage of commitment to marriage. For some people, feelings of tension and anxiety emerge only after they have become officially engaged. For others, these feelings emerge at the first discussion or suggestion of possible engagement.

Age does not seem to be a significant factor. People in their early twenties have suffered from engagement anxiety just as people in their late forties have.

Engagement anxiety can take various forms. In milder cases, you experience nagging doubts and an unwelcome, distressful feeling of hesitation. The normally expected feelings of elation and enthusiastic excitement seem to be missing and you wonder, why?

In some extreme cases, even physical symptoms have been reported. The worry and stress can be so severe that they can lead to loss of appetite, nausea, sleeplessness, inability to concentrate in yeshiva or at work, or even headaches and abdominal pain.

### Since the Time of Adam HaRishon

If you experience any form of engagement anxiety, you may wonder whether you are alone. You may even long for the utopian situation where you would be spared the agonies of having to make this decision. "If I were *Adam HaRishon* (or Chava)," the fantasy goes, "I wouldn't have to worry about whom to marry. The choice would be narrowed to only one candidate!"

Of course, as *Chazal* explain, even Adam and Chava were not spared from the burden of selecting a mate. Rashi explains (*Beraishis* 2:23) that Adam searched among the entire animal kingdom, looking for a mate. The Ramban (*Beraishis* 2:22) sheds some light on the impact of this search on Adam.

> ...[*Hashem*] did not want to take his rib from him [*Adam HaRishon*] until Adam realized that there was no help-mate for him among the creatures and [until] he would yearn to have a helpmate...that was suitable for him...."

So the dilemmas of searching for a proper mate have existed since the time of *Adam HaRishon*. It is also likely that the discomfort and yearning associated with those dilemm..s have existed for almost as long.

Today, engagement anxiety, in some form, is quite common in the Torah community. The legitimate concern with the unacceptably high divorce rate in our community is enough to make almost everyone think twice about proposing or accepting a proposal for marriage.

But is all engagement anxiety the same? Are the different forms of engagement anxiety simply different degrees of the same phenomenon, or are there completely different types?

Indeed, not all engagement anxiety is the same nor should each incidence be treated similarly. There appear to be two distinct types of engagement anxiety: one could be termed "normal" and the other "pathological." While it is often difficult to differentiate between the two types, some general guidelines can be offered.

## Normal Engagement Anxiety

Normal engagement anxiety can manifest itself with both mild as well as severe symptoms of worry, depression, nervousness and preoccupation with doubt. The distinguishing feature of normal engagement anxiety is that the symptoms are brought on by a real and legitimate concern. In addition, the degree of the symptoms is directly related to and appropriate for the seriousness of that concern.

Normal engagement anxiety generally takes one of two forms. Both forms are quite common and, at times, even occur concurrently. Each form can be best described by presenting its typical scenario.

### 1. ADJUSTMENT APPREHENSION

You are satisfied with all aspects of the *shidduch*. In spite of what people were always telling you, you have not had to compromise on any major item on your "checklist" of what you were looking for. You enjoy each other's company very much, and you both respect each other's talents, virtues and accomplishments. In fact, you believe quite firmly that this is your *beshert* (Heavenly ordained match).

In spite of all of this, you are still anxious and worried. Your concerns are not so much related to your *choice* of mate but rather to some aspect of the wedding or marriage, in general. You may be bothered by any of the following questions:

"Will I be fully accepted by my in-laws?"
"Will my friends feel that I did well or poorly in marrying him/her?"
"How well will we adjust to living together?"
"How will I handle the constant spotlight of wedding, *sheva brachos*, etc.?"

As with all forms of engagement anxiety, a private consultation with a trusted *rav*, *rebbe* or mentor would be advisable. Your specific experiences with major adjustments in the past should be explored. Are you someone who always feels apprehensive approaching new situations and new people? Did you feel similarly starting a new yeshiva, seminary, or job?

If the answers to these questions are yes, and if the symptoms of anxiety are relatively mild, then the marriage should really go ahead, as planned. If the symptoms are more severe but the answers to the questions above are still yes, then perhaps a brief and temporary postponement may be helpful. In either case, there is no indication to call off the wedding completely.

The second form of normal engagement anxiety is more problematic and not as easy to deal with.

## 2. CHANCING ON CHANGE

You are pleased with most aspects of the *shidduch*. You enjoy each other's company and you feel comfortable with each other, most of the time. But at other times, there are things about your future mate which really bother you.

You tell yourself that your complaints are foolish, that you are making a big deal over nothing. Sometimes, however, you are not so sure. You tell yourself these things will change. "After marriage," you reassure yourself, "she will settle down and correct these problems." Sometimes, however, you are not so sure. You may be bothered by any of the following questions.

"Will she really change after the wedding, as I want?"
"Will he really change after the wedding, as he promises?"
"Can I accept him as he is and be satisfied in the marriage if he never changes?"

Yes, indeed, people can and do change after marriage. But the change is not always an improvement. Positive change can only come about if the person wants to change himself. If only his spouse wants him to change, the prospects are dimmed considerably.

But don't people change after marriage just to please their spouses? Of course, and in good marriages that goes on continuously, as loving couples grow closer through the years. But to start off a marriage based on an expectation for change is to place the foundation of that marriage on very thin ice. You need to go into marriage with a "What you see is what you get," attitude.

If you are living through this scenario, you should seek out a private consultation with a *rav*, *rebbe* or mentor immediately. Relatively severe symptoms of tension and anxiety accompanying this scenario make the need for an urgent meeting that much more obvious. Together with the *rav*, *rebbe* or mentor, the specific concerns must be examined in a "no-holds-barred" atmosphere of openness and honesty. If the offensive attribute is totally unacceptable, regardless of how insignificant it may seem to others, then serious consideration should be given to breaking the engagement. As painful as that would be, breaking up a marriage and family later would be infinitely more painful. It cannot be overemphasized that many of the people who eventually seek divorces had gone through this form of normal engagement anxiety and were advised to disregard their apprehension and go ahead with the wedding anyway!

Of course, a decision to break an engagement should never be made without first consulting a *rav*. If, after careful deliberation, someone is advised to break an engagement, the need to ask the fiancé for *mechilla* (forgiveness) should not be overlooked.

If it is difficult to decide whether or not the offensive attribute can be accepted as is, then a postponement of the wedding is definitely in order. During the interim, you should continue to see each other. If you do, one of three things will happen: you may decide that you can "live with it" and the marriage plans will proceed; you may decide that you cannot "live with it" and the engagement will be broken off completely; or you may remain chronically undecided. If someone remains undecided about his ability to accept a certain aspect of his fiancé for an extended period, this may signal the presence of pathological engagement anxiety.

### Pathological Engagement Anxiety

Pathological engagement anxiety is much less common than either form of normal engagement anxiety. The symptoms of tension and worry which accompany pathological engagement anxiety may be mild or severe. What distinguishes pathological engagement anxiety from the normal forms is the fact that the concern and worry stem more from internal, chronic and destructive patterns than from genuine reality-based issues. This distinction, of course, is a difficult one to make, even for the most trained and experienced advisor. Nevertheless, the distinction will become clearer as the scenario unfolds.

You are satisfied with all major aspects of the *shidduch*. In spite of the length of your "checklist," you have compromised on no major item. But some of the smaller items are missing. Yes, they are trivialities; you are the first to admit that. But they bother you sometimes. Then, again, at other times you are not bothered at all.

Even more upsetting than what is missing in the *shidduch* is what is missing in yourself. You don't feel excited anymore. You used to, or at least you thought you did. Now the eagerness is gone. You are literally plagued by the following questions which alternate with the intensity of cannon blasts.

"Am I blowing the whole thing out of proportion and risking the loss of my greatest marriage opportunity?"
                    or
"Am I dealing with issues that will continue to bother me, and am I risking a catastrophe if I go ahead with this marriage?"

From this scenario alone, it would still be difficult for friends and relatives to recognize a clear-cut case of pathological engagement anxiety. If you suffer from this malady, however, you have probably already identified yourself in this scenario.

For the friends and relatives, though, three components of pathological engagement anxiety will help to identify this syndrome.

1. *Timetable*: Pathological engagement anxiety is the only form of engagement anxiety which can last for many months. It is even capable of tormenting an individual for years. In some cases, it continues long after the marriage or the break-up.

 **Goldie,** a young engaged woman from a very traditional, Orthodox family, suffered tension and uncertainty for so long that her fiancé gave up on her and finally married someone else. Years later, even after her own marriage to a different man, this woman was still plagued with periodic, recurrent anguish over not having married her first fiancé. Once, when she was expecting her fourth child, she thought she saw her first fiancé on the bus. This incident triggered such intense preoccupational and obsessional thoughts of regret that this woman eventually needed psychotherapy.

2. *Help Seeking Pattern*: Every healthy individual seeks advice from others, at some time. Another distinguishing feature of pathological engagement anxiety, however, is the *manner* in which those who suffer from it seek advice.

Generally, when someone needs advice because they lack information, a survey approach is used. Someone looking to buy a house, for example, who knows absolutely nothing about real estate, will probably consult with many people to gather ideas, tips, and professional opinions. If, on the other hand, someone needs advice because he does not trust his own judgment, one or two opinions will suffice. Someone considering a business partnership, for example, may first consult with one or two trusted *rabbanim* or advisors.

People who suffer from pathological engagement anxiety acknowledge that questions of marriage fall into the second category of judgment decisions. Nevertheless, they are notorious for consulting with far too many people. What is significant here, is not the actual number of times advice is sought, but rather the *manner* in which it is sought. The individual will generally continue to seek out new advisors as if he or she is trying to achieve a balance of 50 percent for and 50 percent against. Ultimately, the advice never calms the individual but only serves to exacerbate the anxiety.

Of course, the individual believes that by seeking advice he can reduce his anxiety and uncertainty. When advice is given, however, the individual finds some minor flaw in the advisor which then nullifies the advice. The individual then seeks another advisor without that flaw. Ultimately, the individual is no more successful in finding a flawless advisor than he or she is in finding a flawless *shidduch*. This "wild goose chase" for "the perfect" advisor not only frustrates the individual but can also wear down the patience of even the most tolerant *rav, rebbe* or mentor.

3. *Correlation with the relationship process*: Given sufficient time, and proper support, normal engagement anxiety can be resolved regardless of the day-to-day interaction between the couple. Here, the anxiety is being aroused by concerns and worries which are relatively unaffected by the presence of the other person. In fact, normal engagement anxiety can be effectively resolved, even when the couple are not seeing each other, such as in Chassidic circles where the couple do not see each other at all during the engagement period.

With pathological engagement anxiety, however, the degree of tension and confusion is directly related to the status of the ongoing relationship. If the other person, for example, even suggests that marriage be discussed, the individual suffering from pathological engagement anxiety will become intensely bothered by some relatively minor aspect of the other person's personality or appearance. If, on the other hand, the other party just intimates that the couple should not continue dating each other exclusively, the individual will become panicky at the thought of losing such an ideal mate. The anxiety is only reduced, therefore, when an *indefinite* status quo is maintained.

 **Mendel,** a yeshiva student, was so panicked at the thought of losing his "best opportunity" that he aggressively pursued a certain seminary graduate each time she gave up on him. After waiting a few months for him to decide, she would grow impatient and break off the relationship in order to date others. He would become so upset by this that he would even wait outside the office where she worked and send messengers to convince her that she should agree to see him again. When she would finally agree, the couple would resume dating and eventually reach the same stalemate. This "on-again, off-again" pattern repeated itself three times within a two-year period.

## The Case of Shaya and Bracha

Perhaps the best way to illustrate the unique features of pathological engagement anxiety would be to present a detailed case example. As with all other case examples in this book, identifying information has been thoroughly disguised in order to protect the privacy of the individuals involved. While in this case it is the young man who suffers from pathological engagement anxiety, women can and do experience the same problems.

 **Shaya** lives in one of the largest American Orthodox Jewish communities. The intensity of his anxiety can be measured by the fact that he consulted with me in person, which involved considerable traveling time and expense in order to get to New York City where I live.

Shaya was employed full-time in his family business after having completed eight years of post-high-school yeshiva study in America and Eretz Yisrael. He had never been married and had been seeing Bracha off and on for a little over one year.

Six months before coming to see me, Shaya initiated a termination of the relationship with Bracha. He had no major complaint other than that he had felt Bracha was not assertive enough. Of course, Shaya admitted that he did not like overly assertive women. But he felt Bracha could be a bit more assertive to suit his taste. He also reported that he "felt nothing" when he was with her. He was fond of her, but on a deep emotional level he felt that something was missing. Bracha was quite attracted to Shaya; but given no alternative, she reluctantly accepted to break up.

For a month and a half, Shaya bitterly sweated out the separation. When it became intolerable, he started seeing Bracha again. Because of the pressure from both families, Shaya could not date Bracha indefinitely, especially after what had happened. To avoid another break-up, Shaya proposed a month later.

Immediately after the engagement became official (he had wanted to keep it *un*official for as long as he could), feelings of panic set in. Shaya feared he was headed for a marital disaster. He did not want to ruin Bracha's life or his own, but he anticipated problems if he would go through with the wedding. On the other hand, he also realized that Bracha was the most compatible young woman he had ever met, and he feared he'd never get married if he passed up this exceptional opportunity.

In desperation, Shaya consulted with a prominent rabbinic leader in his community. Shaya did not know him personally, but the *rav*'s wisdom, insight and Torah knowledge were highly regarded throughout the country. Shaya presented the issues as fully and completely as possible. Although he tried to disguise his request, Shaya basically asked the *rav* whether or not he should go ahead with the wedding. To Shaya's surprise, the *rav* did offer concrete advice: call off the wedding.

Shaya left this meeting with mixed feelings. He appreciated the *rav*'s willingness to commit himself, but he questioned the *rav*'s ability to evaluate the situation. "After all," Shaya reasoned to himself, "how well does the *rav* really understand my personality and my needs?" Because Shaya felt that the *rav*'s advice may have been based on inaccurate first impressions, Shaya felt he needed to consult someone who knew him on a more personal basis. He contacted his former *rosh yeshiva*. The *rosh yeshiva*, of course, did know Shaya quite well, and he was familiar with Shaya's sometimes overly analytical thinking. After more than one lengthy meeting, the *rosh yeshiva* told Shaya to go ahead with the wedding. "A young woman like Bracha," the *rosh yeshiva* argued, "doesn't come along every day."

Although the *rosh yeshiva* gave most generously of his time to Shaya, his advice did not succeed in alleviating Shaya's anxiety. In fact, it only served to increase it. "What an impossible dilemma," Shaya thought, "even these two *gedolim* (Torah giants) are divided on this matter! So how could I ever decide?!"

Shaya felt desperate. It became impossible for him to concentrate at work. He began to lose weight and had difficulty falling asleep at night. He was afraid to share any of this with Bracha for fear she would walk out on him. His mind went around in circles, and he felt trapped, helpless and very frightened. It was at this point that he consulted with me.

During a brief series of intensive sessions, Shaya was helped to face his long-standing difficulty with decision-making. He was then able to see that his current dilemma was a symptom of a more chronic problem. His "choice" of occupation was another excellent example. He had wanted to enter a professional career, but he could not decide between law, accounting, computers or some other unrelated field. His family needed help in the business, so he began working there on a "temporary" basis two years before meeting Bracha. At the time of this writing, Shaya is still unhappily employed in the family business.

These sessions also helped Shaya understand that the emotional closeness which was missing in his relationship with Bracha had been missing in many earlier relationships with friends, *chavrusos* and relatives.

During these sessions, Shaya tried, unsuccessfully, to lure me into advising him about the wedding. Ultimately Shaya did reluctantly acknowledge his need for additional professional help to resolve his chronic fears of failure and crippling indecisiveness.

Why couldn't Shaya be given advice about the wedding? After all, wasn't that what he was really after? Had Shaya been told to go ahead with the wedding, he would have taken that to mean that there was at least a good chance for the marriage to succeed. His chronic indecisiveness and fear of commitment, however, precluded a blissful marriage. Had Shaya been told to break off the engagement, he would have taken that to mean there was at least a good chance that he would find a better *shidduch*. Considering how many girls he had dated before meeting Bracha, however, who could offer him that reassurance?

However, I did advise Shaya to postpone his wedding, to relieve some of the decision-making pressure. Shaya completely rejected that advice and repeatedly tried to manipulate me into making the commitment which he himself could not make and which, when made by two *gedolim*, did not alleviate any of Shaya's anxiety at all.

Shaya finally decided to go ahead with the marriage although his terrifying agony continued beyond the very end of the eleventh hour. As is typical of those who suffer from pathological engagement anxiety, he has been unable to accept his own decision. Shaya was convinced that he had made the wrong decision, which is what would have happened either way. Since the wedding, he has been tormented with regret and guilt which constantly plague him. He did accept my referral, however, and is engaged in a more ongoing therapeutic relationship in his home town. At the time of this writing, Shaya was questioning the expertise and appropriateness of his current therapist, but not his need for therapy.

Although Shaya's case is, indeed, quite extreme, it is not at all uncommon. Unfortunately there are more Shayas who are torturing themselves and their Brachas. If they, their friends, and their relatives are able to recognize the symptoms of pathological engagement anxiety, some of their frustration and suffering may be reduced.

In cases of pathological engagement anxiety, for example, advice on the marriage never helps. Discussions of the pros and cons of a particular *shidduch* are useless. In fact, there really is nothing that can be done right away for these people to help them make a decision about marriage which they will be able to fully accept, without regret, doubt or hesitation. Certainly these people can be helped to overcome their problems but only after they acknowledge the problems, and not overnight.

For some people, as was the case with Shaya, the long-standing problems are more or less manageable throughout adolescence and young adulthood. Only at the point of marital engagement do the problems surface with their full intensity. For others, the self-doubt, indecisiveness and fear of failure are more readily apparent at earlier stages. If these young people were helped in time, they might reach dating and courtship with their problems well behind them.

## Summary and Conclusions

Some degree of anxiety is quite common among *bnai* and *bnos Torah* as they approach their wedding days. In most cases the anxiety is temporary and unrelated to the choice of marital partner. This anxiety usually passes with time, patience and encouragement.

In other cases, the anxiety is directly related to specific concerns and questions about the choice of marital partner. If these questions are ignored or belittled, the anxiety may be suppressed temporarily, only to surface later, when the consequences are more severe. Facing these questions openly and honestly does not necessarily result in a canceled or even postponed wedding. Facing these questions, however, is the most constructive approach with the greatest long-term benefit. If the decision is made to go ahead with the wedding, the *chassan* or *kalla* in question will approach the *chuppa* more eagerly, without the burden of tension and doubt.

Finally, in a few, not insignificant cases, the engagement anxiety signals a long-standing psychological problem which will prove to be stubbornly unresponsive to logical advice and counsel. In these cases, very little can be done to resolve the immediate dilemma regarding the wedding, and often only professional help can address the underlying psychological problem.

Certainly considerable training and experience is necessary in order to help those who suffer from pathological engagement anxiety. But every anxious *chassan* or *kalla* will benefit if their friends, relatives and *rebbe'im* do not lump engagement anxiety together, assuming that it always requires the same approach. While differentiating between one form of engagement anxiety and another may, at times, be a task for experts, becoming familiar with the existence of different forms of engagement anxiety may be an obligation for all parents, *mechanchim* and *rebbe'im* in order to properly fulfill the Torah prohibition "not to place a stumbling block before the blind" (*Vayikra* 19:14).

The *Sefer HaChinnuch* (*siman* 232) explains that included in this *mitzva* is the prohibition against giving any bad advice. The *Sefer HaChinnuch* goes on to elaborate on the basis of this *mitzva*:

> It is well known that the perfection of the world is achieved
> through guiding people and giving them appropriate
> advice for all their needs.

The *Sefer HaChinnuch* concludes that this *mitzva* "applies everywhere, at all times, to men and women." And whoever gives his fellow Jew "advice which is not proper... is like someone who has violated the command of the King."

Everyone knows that the *chuppa* represents a dual milestone. The *chuppa* signifies the termination of the *chassan*'s and *kalla*'s single life, and it also marks the beginning of the couple's new married life together. In a similar vein, then, the wedding testifies to the couple's successful passage through the turbulence of dating, courtship and engagement. The wedding also places the couple at the threshold of marriage itself with all of its new opportunities and new challenges.

While marriage presents new opportunities and new challenges throughout life, "until a hundred and twenty," perhaps the most challenging period for the vast majority of couples is the first year of marriage.

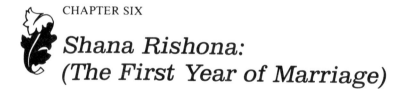

# CHAPTER SIX

# Shana Rishona: (The First Year of Marriage)

There are some very basic trouble spots in marriage that tend to crop up most often during the *shana rishona* (the first year). If you are aware of these potential problem areas, you stand a better chance of avoiding them, in line with the maxim, "Who is wise, he who sees [i.e. anticipates] the future" (*Tamid* 32a).

The term *shana rishona*, of course, should not be taken literally. The problems outlined here may be encountered by some couples right after marriage, while others may struggle with these issues for many years. The point is that these problems generally surface during the initial adjustment phase of marriage, which typically lasts one year. As the *Sefer HaChinnuch* points out (*Parshas Ki Saisai, siman* 582), the first year of marriage is the critical phase during which the couple develops a strong attachment.

While there are at least as many different problems that can confront a young couple as there are young couples, there are six major problem areas which can develop in marriage during the *shana rishona*.

## Impatience and Stubbornness

Some young married men and women have a very short-sighted timetable for change, growth and adjustment.

These people believe that if their spouse does not make immediate concessions to their way of thinking, they lose all hopes of negotiating the issue in the future, as though marriage were a political struggle with wins and losses.

Most often, the issue is quite insignificant, as both partners acknowledge. It only becomes an issue because one or both spouses believe that their entire future is at stake.

If this problem area sounds a bit far-fetched to you, try to imagine yourself in the following case.

 **Devora** and **Heschie** were married three months before Pesach. As *yom tov* approached, they began discussing their holiday plans. Heschie assumed that they would spend *yom tov* with his parents, who were scheduled to move out of town right after Pesach. Devora insisted that traditionally the first *yom tov* "belongs" to the wife's parents. Heschie agreed, but since his parents would thereafter be living out of town, perhaps Devora should give in. Devora saw a principle here that was much larger than the question at hand. She felt that unless she stood firm on this issue her husband would "walk all over her" in the future.

Heschie and Devora are still married and are not even considering a divorce. The resentment generated by their initial intransigence, however, still surfaces today, almost five years later.

Of course, Devora was right. Traditionally, a newly married couple does spend the first *yom tov* with the wife's family. But Heschie was also right. Since his parents would soon be moving out of town, perhaps he and Devora should spend Pesach with his parents.

The issue here was not which spouse had the valid position. They both did. The issue here was how much each one was willing to risk for the sake of "principle." In this case, both Heschie and Devora were willing to put their *shalom bayis* on the line for the sake of "principle."

Because neither Heschie nor Devora was willing to compromise, a relatively minor issue mushroomed into a major source of conflict. What Heschie and Devora should have learned *before* they got married was that being right and having your way are not the most important things in life and certainly not in marriage. Had they learned that lesson, perhaps they would have been somewhat more flexible with each other. Then the entire issue would never have become an "issue" in the first place.

Heschie and Devora's behavior could best be compared to the driver who had the right of way and therefore refused to yield to an oncoming truck. After the collision, all witnesses at the scene agreed that the driver of the car was right — he was *dead* right.

## Protection through Silence

The advice of *Chazal* is full of injunctions to remain silent. Some interpret *baishanim* (see page 55) to refer to modest reticence. In contrast, one of the popular attitudes today, which is most antithetical to Torah, can be summarized by the hackneyed cliché, "Express yourself!" We certainly do not believe that every thought and emotion must be shared openly with the entire world. On the contrary, a person should strive to internalize the external restraint and refinement that he exhibits. In secular society, people try to achieve just the opposite by "letting it all hang out."

Nevertheless, there are certain situations in which excessive silence can be destructive. Silence, like any other ideal, must be kept in perspective. In an unreasonable effort to emulate his impression of *gedolim*, a young married person may weaken the entire foundation of his married life.

**Rachel** and **Aryeh** are a good example. When they first got married, some of Rachel's habits disturbed Aryeh. While he could accept most of these habits, one really annoyed him. It was nothing unusual, but Aryeh's reaction created a major rift that still exists today.

Often when Aryeh would be leaving the apartment, Rachel would remember something that she wanted to tell him. Even if he was rushing out the door, late for *minyan*, a *shiur* or just an appointment, Rachel would insist that Aryeh wait briefly until she told him what she had just remembered.

Every time this occurred, Aryeh reminded himself of Talmudic injunctions to remain silent, and with great self-control he suppressed his impulse to criticize Rachel.

Aryeh felt very noble about his self-sacrifice. After all, he was avoiding conflict and was sparing his wife the displeasure of being criticized. "If I point this out to Rachel," he reasoned, "it could lead to argument."

In a way, Aryeh's reasoning was valid. He certainly should have tried to overlook his wife's human imperfections. Unnecessary criticism and possible conflict should be avoided. In fact, you may even admire Aryeh. And based on the case history reported thus far, you might assume that Aryeh acted wisely.

Nevertheless, Aryeh made two big mistakes. First, he assumed that Rachel would be hurt if she knew that one of her habits offended him. Actually, she wanted nothing more than to please Aryeh. Had she been told openly, she probably would have changed her behavior immediately.

Aryeh's second mistake was much more serious. He thought that he would eventually get used to this habit and come to accept it. He was wrong. As time went on, it bothered him more and more, until he started wondering why Rachel didn't realize *on her own* that he was annoyed by her habit. At that point, the die was cast. His annoyance quickly grew into resentment. The harder he tried to control the resentment, the angrier Aryeh became.

Finally, after seven months, Aryeh exploded. His burst of temper was set off by a small, irrelevant incident, but he raised his voice and used strong language quite unbefitting a *ben Torah*.

The outburst did clear the air somewhat, but Aryeh felt so guilty about it that he was more determined than ever to keep quiet. Rachel, of course, was shocked and hurt. She felt that she had failed to please her husband and worried about their future.

For the next eleven years, Aryeh and Rachel's marriage was strained with occasional violent outbursts. Finally, they sat down with a counselor and began to unravel their tangled feelings. When they were through, they realized how Aryeh's overly zealous efforts "to look away" from his wife's faults had led into a disastrous chain of events, which fortunately was finally resolved.

Certainly Aryeh's misguided effort to remain silent was not the sole cause of his marital problems. Complex marital and family problems seldom stem from one simple source. Nevertheless, if Aryeh had realized that his efforts to remain silent could do more harm than good, much of his and Rachel's unhappiness could have been prevented.

So if your spouse says or does something that disturbs or upsets you, ask yourself the following question, "Can I honestly overlook this?" If the answer is yes, then by all means do so. But if the answer is no (and here you must be completely open and truthful with yourself), then you must sit down with your spouse and calmly, *tactfully* discuss whatever bothers you. Remember, if you try to fool yourself, as Aryeh did, you will only repeat his mistakes instead of learning from them.

## Corrosive Competition

Every *mechanaich* knows that competition can foster motivation and achievement in the classroom. But competition is a two-sided coin. And every *mechanaich* knows that competition can also lead to rivalry, jealousy and resentment which can be most destructive. Ultimately, the more experienced *mechanchim* realize that competition in the classroom can never be eliminated, but it can be monitored and controlled to produce the optimum atmosphere which promotes learning and personality growth.

While competition may be potentially constructive in the classroom, it is only destructive in the area of *shidduchim* and marriage. We need to look no further than to the larger, Western society around us to see numerous examples of the corrosive influence of competition in marriage. In fact, for many people in the secular society, marriage represents the ultimate arena of competition. These people do not see their spouses as partners in life but rather as a means to achieve status, praise and recognition from others.

Unfortunately, some of these attitudes may creep into our community as well. If this happens, you might hear people talking about *shidduchim* and spouses in terms which come dangerously close to violating the Tenth Commandment (*Shmos* 20:4).

If you hear comments such as, "She's not as pretty as my cousin's *kalla*," or "He doesn't have as good a job as my best friend's *chassan*," then you should suspect feelings of competition.

And if you hear comments such as, "My husband doesn't diaper the baby nearly as often as my upstairs neighbor's husband," or "My wife never seems to handle the children as well as my *chavrusa*'s (study partner's) wife," then you know that feelings of competition are beginning to corrode these marriages.

**Baila** and **Alex** got married shortly before Rosh Hashana. Since Alex used up his vacation days at work for the wedding and *sheva brachos,* he had to "borrow" against next summer's vacation to take off for *yom tov.* So when the summer rolled around, Alex and Baila made what seemed to be the most logical plans for a vacation. They rented a bungalow in the country.

In July, Alex took Baila and their month-old baby up to the bungalow colony. He returned to "the City" every Monday morning to go to work. Fridays he came up to the bungalow, and once in a while he even managed to come up Thursday night.

Alex and Baila were hesitant about this arrangement. They each expressed apprehension about the impact of the long separation each week. But they decided that just because Alex couldn't get away was no reason to keep Baila and the baby cooped up in their tiny, stuffy apartment. Even if they did miss each other very much, they agreed, "The absence would just make the heart grow fonder."

At first, Alex and Baila really enjoyed the bungalow colony. They made many new friends and they both enjoyed the relaxed atmosphere that prevailed. They were pleased with their decision.

During the week, Baila and Alex did miss each other but kept in touch by phone and counted the days until Friday. If Baila did feel lonely, she never had far to go to find a friend or two or three with whom to chat. Baila, therefore, had more than ample opportunity to observe her neighbors. After three weeks, it began to take its toll.

It was their regularly scheduled Wednesday night phone call. Because it was long distance, they had to keep the conversation brief and each word was measured. At the end of the call Baila added the following request, "Maybe you could come up tomorrow night?"

"I'd love to," Alex responded, "but you know I came up last week on Thursday night, and I really had to pay for it on Monday. You know how hard it is to take off an extra day when you're in computers."

"I know you always say that, but Chavi's husband and Shani's husband are both in computers, too, and they come up *every* Thursday night!"

That's how it started. As the summer wore on, Baila also threw up to Alex how he did not bring flowers each Friday like Suri's husband, drive into town *motza'ai Shabbos* like Chavie's husband, or make barbecues as adeptly as Shani's husband. Of course, all of the references to Suri, Chavi and Shani got Alex to thinking about how these women never seemed to criticize their husbands as much as Baila was doing.

By the end of August, both Baila and Alex regretted their decision to spend the summer at a bungalow colony. Seeing the other couples so happily married (at least that's how they appeared) made their own conflicts that much more upsetting.

Baila and Alex continued to criticize and attack each other, long after the summer. They also continued to throw up to each other examples of various "model" spouses. The bitterness even led them to the brink of divorce, which was only prevented by some very intensive marriage counseling.

How can you learn from Alex and Baila's mistakes and prevent your *shana rishona* from becoming the fiasco it was for them?

First and foremost, you must heed the advice of the Ibn Ezra (*Shmos* 20:14). How can a person resist *desiring* something appealing even though it does not belong to him? The Ibn Ezra explains with his famous parable of the villager who sees the daughter of the king pass by. Even though she is a beautiful princess, he would no sooner long to marry her than he would long for wings to be able to fly. So, too, a person must view someone else's spouse as equally off limits.

"But I don't want to marry anyone else. I just want my spouse to achieve the same good looks, wealth, or character traits as someone else. What's wrong with that?" you might ask.

So if the words of Ibn Ezra are not helpful to you, reflect on the advice of Hillel, "Do not judge your neighbor until you are in his place" (*Pirkai Avos* 2:4). Although the primary intent of this teaching is to give a wrongdoer the benefit of the doubt, this teaching can be applied, perhaps, to "judging" your neighbor's spouse as well. In other words, just because your friend's spouse *seems* so generous, affectionate, and helpful to your friend in public does not mean that that is always the case at home. Just as your spouse makes a better impression in public, your neighbor's spouse does as well.

So remember this: If you view marriage as a race to "keep up" with your friends and you push your spouse to match up to the attractive and appealing attributes of your friends' spouses, you will end up finishing last, losing the only prize that really counts — *shalom bayis.*

## Passing the Tests

Everyone comes to marriage with a long shopping list of expectations, hopes, and dreams. That is as it should be, for these expectations provide the incentives that help single people take the plunge into marriage.

These lists are all unique and highly personalized. Nevertheless, there is one item that is probably at the top of your list, whether or not you are aware of it: to be loved and cared for by your spouse.

No, there is nothing wrong or unusual about that expectation. Some people, however, also come to marriage with a large suitcase full of self-doubt, insecurity, and low self-esteem. Even though they desperately want to be loved and cared for, deep inside they believe that they are so unworthy and inadequate that no one could ever really love or care for them.

One could assume that their spouses do care for them, or they would not have married them. Yet in spite of any expression of caring from their spouses, these people feel the need "to test" them.

This may sound farfetched, but, then again, have you ever heard someone say, "If he really cared about me, he would _____!" Such a statement and all its variations indicate that one spouse is testing the other, that the care and concern of one's spouse can only be measured by the criterion of doing this or not doing that.

Sometimes these criteria are valid. No one would take issue with, "If he really cared about me, he wouldn't insult me like that in front of my friends!" By contrast, consider this criterion: "If she really cared about me, she wouldn't have put so much mustard on this sandwich!" No, not too many men would make such a statement. But many young married men and women have similar *thoughts* about their spouses, and such thoughts drive a wedge between husband and wife that can lead to irreconcilable differences.

 **Mordechai** and **Faigie's** eighteen-year-old marriage was riddled with the scars of constant testing. The complete list of their mutual failures to trust each other could fill volumes. One illustration, however, will suffice.

Mordechai worked long hours as a junior partner in a large accounting firm. He would have preferred to keep more reasonable hours but felt pressured to put in the same "overtime" as the other junior partners. So when Mordechai decided that it would be a good idea to have a safety-deposit box, he felt it was a reasonable request to ask Faigie to make the arrangements at their local bank. "After all," Mordechai reasoned, "Faigie finishes teaching at 2 P.M. every day. Surely she should find time to take care of this."

Faigie didn't feel that a safety-deposit box was so important. In addition, she wasn't a very organized person and didn't get to things right away.

Whenever Mordechai asked about the safety-deposit box, he kept getting the same reply from Faigie, "I didn't have a chance yet." This began to irritate Mordechai, who felt, "If Faigie really wanted to please me, she would have taken care of this already." He eventually started to nag her about it.

Of course, Mordechai could have taken care of this errand himself, too. But he felt that Faigie should do it, and he wanted to prove to himself that she did care about him. After a while he stopped nagging, but he still did not arrange for the safety-deposit box himself.

What about Faigie? What was getting in her way? At first, she simply forgot. When Mordechai started nagging, this became a test for her, too. "I'd like to see," she thought to herself, "whether Mordechai is going to let a silly thing like this affect his feelings for me." Even after Mordechai gave up and stopped nagging she thought, "I'd like to see how long he can really hold out before he starts nagging again!"

The issue did resurface about one year later. Mordechai and Faigie's apartment was burglarized. All of their appliances and jewelry were stolen, much of which was not yet insured (another one of Faigie's "responsibilities"). Mordechai blamed Faigie for the jewelry losses since she had still not arranged for the safety-deposit box.

Renting a safety-deposit box really *is* a small errand. In this regard both Mordechai and Faigie were correct. But the way each one used this as an opportunity to test the other's degree of caring was most destructive.

In order to steer clear of Faigie and Mordechai's problem of testing, you need to remember that once you start setting up little tests to measure your spouse's caring, you are planting the seeds for reaping a bumper crop of marital problems.

If you are feeling uncertain about your spouse's level of concern and caring for you, bring it up. While it may disturb your spouse to hear it, at least it will be brought into the open and can then be dealt with directly. But if you keep your concern to yourself and you try to reassure yourself by testing your spouse, you are likely to fall into the same trap as Faigie and Mordechai.

## In-Law Interference

Another frequent and destructive cause of marital conflict during the *shana rishona* is premature and inappropriate interference by the parents of the wife, the husband, or both.

As has been stressed here repeatedly, parents do have an important role to play in preparing their children for successful marriages. That parental role, of course, does not terminate once you begin dating. Hopefully, it will continue for a lifetime, providing an invaluable source of sage advice.

But if parents are supposed to provide their advice throughout the process of dating, courtship and marriage, at what point does "advice" become "interference"? Furthermore, how can you tell when the interference is "constructive," which will forestall a tragedy, or "destructive," which will create one?

In answering these questions, two general guidelines can be offered in the form of questions. These are questions which you must ask yourself as you try to evaluate the role your parents are playing in your dating, courtship or marriage. The first question applies more to the dating and courtship phase while the second question deals with the *shana rishona.*

1. To what extent do you feel your parents are motivated by concern for your needs or their own needs?

In order to accept your parents' interference as constructive you must be reasonably confident that your parents have your interests uppermost in their minds. Your parents will probably always assure you that they do. But if you have any doubts, do not hesitate to consult with an independent third party, such as a *rav, rebbe* or *mechanaich.*

Although it may sound extreme, the following case is unembellished and illustrates a rather clear case of parental interference which was most destructive.

 **Esther** and **Avi** both came from families who believed that *shidduchim* must be approved by the parents before the couple meet each other. So it was only after they and their families were "checked out" that Avi and Esther met for the first time. Once they finally saw each other, both Esther and Avi knew that this was "it!"

As enthusiastic as they were about the *shidduch*, neither Avi nor Esther wanted to rush into anything. So they controlled themselves and took things one step at a time. On each successive date, they discussed more and more serious topics until they each knew intuitively that they would become engaged.

Although Avi had met Esther's parents, she had not yet formally met his parents. In fact, Avi had been rather thoroughly interviewed by Esther's older brother and father when he came to Esther's house for the first time. But Avi and Esther knew that nothing could be official until Avi's parents met Esther.

In some ways, Avi was even more anxious about that meeting than Esther was. He feared considerable embarrassment if his parents would reject Esther now after having agreed to the *shidduch* in theory and after his own decision to go this far.

To the relief of all, Avi's parents were totally delighted with Esther, and they gave the couple their blessing. Avi and Esther, however, were still not officially engaged. According to the protocol which was accepted and understood by both families, Avi and Esther could only become officially engaged after one final step: a meeting between both sets of parents.

By now, of course, Esther and Avi considered themselves very much engaged, albeit unofficially. They certainly did not announce their engagement to their friends, but close relatives were sure that their engagement was imminent.

The next *Motza'ai Shabbos*, Avi and his parents came to Esther's home. The two sets of parents sat down together and encouraged Esther and Avi to leave, which they did gladly. At this point, they were grateful for any time they could be with each other alone.

Avi and Esther went out for a deliciously long walk. They spoke of marriage plans and trivialities, both of which intensified their commitment to each other. When they returned they expected to drink the traditional *l'chayim*, making the engagement official.

There was no *l'chayim*. When Esther and Avi returned they immediately read the painful expressions on their parents' faces. Something had gone wrong. No explanations were given. The *shidduch* was being called off. Avi's parents insisted that he leave with them at once, which he did most reluctantly.

Avi and Esther never did become engaged. In spite of vigorous efforts to pry loose the information, neither Avi nor Esther ever found out exactly what transpired between their parents that evening. Esther, however, did succeed in obtaining a partial account.

According to her parents, the disagreement centered around which set of parents would be responsible for purchasing the couple a set of bedroom furniture. Avi's parents offered to pay for a dining room set but insisted that Esther's parents agree to purchase a bedroom set worth at least $5,000. Esther's parents agreed to assist the couple financially but were incensed that their daughter's acceptability was being determined by such materialistic criteria.

To say that Avi and Esther were shocked and disappointed would be a gross understatement. They were devastated! Nevertheless, they both loved and respected their parents. Once their parents called off the *shidduch*, they each just accepted it as not *beshert* (Heavenly ordained).

Could it not be argued that both sets of parents had their children's interests foremost in their minds? Perhaps. But I suspect that at least one set of parents was more motivated by personal pride and self-interest.

I certainly hope that Avi and Esther have each gotten married by now. But it is entirely possible that one or both are still looking. If so, it would make it all the more unfortunate that they did not marry each other.

But at least you may be able to learn from their mistake. If you suspect that your parents are interfering in your dating, courtship or marriage in a way which is counterproductive, don't acquiesce, automatically. What you should do is suggest, respectfully of course, that perhaps a *gadol* (Torah giant) should be consulted. In that way you can insure that any parental interference is truly constructive.

The next question deals more directly with the *shana rishona*.

2. To what extent is the parental involvement agreed upon by both spouses?

Once a couple gets married, they do not sever, *chas v'shalom*, their ties with their parents. Nevertheless, certain boundaries of privacy do need to be respected by both husband and wife. If these boundaries are violated, considerable resentment can be generated.

**Shalom** and **Zahava** had such a problem. Zahava had always been close with both of her parents, even though she always considered herself very independent. Shalom was much less involved with his own parents, or least that's how he saw it.

During their first year of marriage, Zahava and Shalom had a number of heated arguments. Shalom had a quick temper and often said things he regretted later. Zahava was very hurt and usually turned to her mother for support. When Shalom discovered that Zahava was reporting the details of each marital dispute to her mother, he was so enraged that he even considered ending the marriage.

Shalom argued that what went on between him and Zahava was private. He resented being asked questions by his mother-in-law that indicated she knew even the most intimate details of the couple's married life.

Zahava felt disadvantaged and helpless. She felt so hurt and crushed by Shalom's verbal attacks that she needed support from somebody.

Certainly Shalom did have a problem controlling his temper. His verbal outbursts were totally unacceptable. Nevertheless, that did not give Zahava license to violate the couple's privacy. By doing so, she only succeeded in making a bad situation worse.

Should you, therefore, never consult with parents or outsiders if you have a marital problem? Of course you should, but not without first discussing the need to do so with your spouse.

Perhaps this advice has been articulated best by HaRav Shlomo Wolbe in his *Kuntrais Hadracha L'Kallos* (Guidance booklet for brides). As HaRav Wolbe put it (my own translation), "A man and woman must exercise modesty not only in dressing. One principle that a couple must adhere to rigorously if they hope to achieve success in marriage is that under no circumstances should they discuss any matter pertaining to each other with anyone. This is a jurisdiction that no one has the right to enter. Whether they are parents, relatives or close friends, when it comes to matters between you and your spouse, keep it private. If a question does arise, turn to the right person: a *rav*, or a *gadol* who can give proper advice... And if, occasionally, a couple does require parental advice, this should only be sought with the prior agreement of husband and wife" (p. 25).

## Childbirth and Its Aftereffects

There is perhaps no greater blessing that Heaven can bestow upon a young married couple than the birth of a child. Many fortunate couples receive that blessing before the end of their *shana rishona*. Other couples are not blessed with children right away. But whether children are born sooner or later, they are always welcomed into a Torah home by their parents with a combination of joy, excitement and a sense of fulfillment.

Sometimes, however, the arrival of children into a marriage is seen as a somewhat mixed blessing. A newborn child certainly brings *simcha* into a Jewish home. But a newborn child also imposes added pressures, responsibilities and restrictions on the parents.

For most couples, the added responsibilities of parenting are a small price to pay for the joy of having children. For some couples, however, these additional responsibilities can even lead to marital tension.

All of this is true whenever a child is born. But when that child is the first child, the impact is even more dramatic. At the outset, you were a dating *couple*, then an engaged *couple* and finally a married *couple*. But now you are a *family*. So when your twosome becomes a threesome that shift can send shock waves through even the most stable marriage.

Many of the old schedules, patterns of behavior and even life-styles need to be replaced with ones that can accommodate the needs of the newborn. The family income needs to be allocated differently to cover the new expenditures. Family visits, vacations and just shopping trips now require more complicated planning. Even the quiet moments alone are now reduced by the very unpredictable crying of the newborn baby.

Of course, none of this is unusual or unmanageable, and no one needs to feel overwhelmed. In most cases, couples make the necessary adjustments without any fuss or fanfare. In some cases, however, these adjustments become monumental challenges which are not so easily overcome. For these couples, the challenges of child care become nothing less than a crisis.

 **Eliyahu** and **Nechama** had a storybook courtship and engagement. They met each other through a series of most unusual circumstances. A few dates later they became engaged and easily weathered some minor in-law and extended-family disputes involving the wedding. Their *shana rishona* was more or less as blissful as their courtship and engagement...until the baby was born.

A few weeks after the baby was born, Eli confided to Nechama that he was concerned about a "sensation" he felt in his stomach. Nechama already knew not to take Eli's somatic complaints too seriously, and she dismissed it as indigestion. Eli repeated his concern the next day, and Nechama again disregarded it.

By the third day, Nechama finally suggested that Eli take a non-prescription antacid, which he did. By the end of the week, however, even Nechama was getting concerned. So she suggested that Eli go for a medical check-up.

Eli received a complete bill of good health from his

doctor, but he was still concerned about the "sensations" in his stomach. After all, he wondered, if nothing is wrong, why should I be having these "sensations."

Against his better judgment, and perhaps just to protect himself, Eli's doctor told him that he could go for "further tests" if he wanted. The doctor assured Eli that he did not believe these tests were necessary, and since they were very expensive and required Eli to be hospitalized he was not recommending them. Nevertheless, if he wanted to be "absolutely certain" that nothing was wrong he could go into the hospital for the tests. Eli wanted the tests.

At this point, Nechama could not take any more. How much reassurance did Eli need?! She was convinced that Eli was just "talking it into himself." She insisted that he just forget about it. Didn't she have enough to handle with the new baby? Did she need Eli to be moping around the house depressed and anxious about his imaginary illness?

After an extremely heated discussion, Nechama finally agreed to a compromise. They would consult their *rav* and follow his advice. The *rav* listened very carefully and finally concluded that it would be *assur* for Eli to subject himself to this unnecessary testing. Nechama was relieved. But Eli continued to brood.

Finally, at her wits end, Nechama suggested that Eli consult a therapist. To her surprise, the therapist requested to see her together with Eli. The therapist took a detailed history of the couple's escalating crisis. He then asked what seemed to be an irrelevant question.

"Eli," the therapist asked, "how attentive to you has Nechama been since the baby was born?"

"Well," Eli began haltingly, "she has been very busy with the baby." Then he quickly added, "But I understand that the baby comes first."

The therapist eventually learned that Eli was feeling somewhat left out of Nechama's life, and in some ways he felt replaced by the baby. The therapist then told them that such feelings are common, and he encouraged the couple to hire a baby-sitter and spend some time together, which they hadn't done since the baby was born.

By the time the couple returned for their next appointment two weeks later, Eli hardly felt his "sensations" and had decided not to go for the hospital tests.

Eli and Nechama's example may sound somewhat extreme. Nevertheless, there are two things you can learn from this case.

First, you need to expect that your spouse may not be able to give you the same amount of time and attention after your first baby is born, as he or she did before. This applies to both men and women. Just as with natural childbirth lessons, if you are prepared for what's coming, you are better able to handle it.

Second, you need to try to balance the baby's needs with your own. Certainly the baby's needs do come first; but if yours never come at all, your marriage will eventually suffer. So no matter how thin your budget is stretched by the birth of your first child, you simply must set aside a few dollars for baby-sitting. You don't have to go out to an expensive restaurant every week. Even if it's just for a leisurely walk, you and your spouse need *some* time alone with each other — without the baby.

If you familiarize yourself with the six most common problem areas that can crop up during the *shana rishona*, you and your spouse stand a good chance of steering clear of these pitfalls. It is certainly no guarantee, but just by reviewing the mistakes of others, summarized here, you increase the likelihood that you will be able to avoid those same mistakes.

But this small book could not possibly contain examples of all the potential problem areas and sources of conflict in marriage. Problems related to the intimate aspects of marriage, for example, have been deliberately omitted here in deference to the tenets of *tznius*. So even if you review this book until you practically know it by heart, it will not insure that your dating, courtship and marriage will be problem free. Therefore, it is quite probable that you will encounter a problem in dating or marriage which is not covered here and which you cannot solve by yourselves. If and when that happens, you will need the advice provided in the next chapter.

# CHAPTER SEVEN

# When <u>You</u> Need Help

After HaRav Avrohom Pam, *shlita* , reviewed the manuscript for this book, he offered only one criticism. There was something very important which he felt had been omitted. HaRav Pam, *shlita*, advised that the book include strong encouragement for people to seek help for marital problems before they escalate into irreconcilable differences. He cited numerous examples from his vast experience of cases in which relatively minor problems grew to unsolvable proportions because one or both spouses stubbornly resisted seeking help until it was too late.

In response to the advice of HaRav Pam, *shlita*, therefore, the next three chapters have been added. This chapter will address the following question: How do you know when outside help is necessary?

## When to Get Help

Not every problem requires an immediate solution, and not every unmet need constitutes an emergency. Small children, however, cannot differentiate between the trivial and the significant. In addition, their tolerance level for frustration is extremely low. That is why most of their requests sound more like demands. After all, they are only children. But as children mature into adults, hopefully they learn to separate the trivial from the significant, while they also expand their frustration tolerance.

It is well understood, therefore, that being able to live with an unsolved problem is a sign of maturity. It is also well accepted that another sign of maturity is not "making mountains out of molehills."

As you enter marriage, however, these distinctions are not so easily made. Since you don't have an extensive background of personal experience, you lack a solid frame of reference with which to make these judgments. As a result, you may find yourself troubled by one of the following dilemmas:

> "Perhaps I'm making a big deal over nothing. But then, again, maybe this is an important issue which needs to be addressed now before it's too late."

or

> "Perhaps I should accept things as they are, at least for the time being, and let the situation resolve itself, gradually. On the other hand, maybe the situation will never resolve itself and it would be foolish not to seek outside help now."

While these dilemmas may arise at any stage of marriage, they are much more likely to arise during the first few years of married life. When these questions do come up, are there any guidelines for answering them? Or, more bluntly, how do you know when outside help is really needed?

Two criteria can be used for deciding whether outside help is necessary. The first relates to the problem itself, and the second deals more with the efforts made to solve the problem.

### SERIOUSNESS OF THE PROBLEM

There is no absolute, objective catalogue of marital problems. Certainly it would make things a lot easier for couples in conflict if one existed. Then all you would have to do is look up your problem in the index and check whether the problem was rated as "serious" or "trivial."

The reason no one has yet published such an inventory of marital problems is because the seriousness of a marital problem is purely subjective. So what is serious to you may be insignificant to your friend. But the fact that your friend may be able to overlook the same issue does not make it any less serious for you.

Therefore, the first criterion you must use in deciding whether outside help is needed is how much you are bothered by the problem. More specifically, you should be asking yourself the following questions:

How often do I think about this problem?
How often does this problem come up?
How badly do I feel when the problem arises?
Has this marital problem affected me in other areas of my life?

Then use your answers as a guide. For example, if you ruminate over the problem daily, if it comes up at least once a week, if you are so upset at times that you feel like crying, and if your concentration and performance at work or learning are impaired, then you should consider your marital problem serious enough to require outside help.

But if you think about the problem only once in a while; if it barely comes up once every two or three months, if you are not even upset enough to feel like complaining to a friend, and if your problem does not affect you at all in other areas, then you should consider your problem too insignificant to warrant a call for help.

Yes, of course, there is a huge gray area in between these two extremes. But the main point here is that you should be measuring the seriousness of your problem by how badly *you* feel about it and how severely it affects *you*.

So if you are very bothered about something in your marriage, then you may need some outside help. Remember, if you hold back from getting help because you're afraid someone else would not be concerned if he were in your place, then you may end up postponing getting help until it's too late.

### FAILURE AT PROBLEM SOLVING

If you have a marital problem which really bothers you, seeking outside help should never be your first effort to solve the problem. So if you haven't tried anything else yet, postpone getting outside help.

What should you try first? The first steps you should take are so obvious that it is almost superfluous to mention them. Nevertheless, since we live in an age when much that is obvious gets overlooked (see Introduction to *Mesillas Yesharim*), a brief outline of problem solving strategies will be presented here.

— Try to sit down with your spouse to discuss the problem. Is your spouse aware of the problem? How does your spouse understand it? What solutions could he recommend? Be sure to include your own thoughts and feelings in the discussion.

During this discussion be sure to avoid the three most common pitfalls which sabotage any marital problem solving session: don't exaggerate or minimize your feelings (i.e., say what you really mean); don't bring in tangential issues (i.e., stick to the main points); and don't jump to any premature conclusions about your spouse's intentions, feelings or motives (i.e., ask your spouse what he meant instead of guessing).

If repeated efforts to discuss the problem with your spouse have failed, there is still something else you can do.

— Try to sit down with yourself to visualize the problem from your spouse's point of view. Sure you've thought about the problem a lot already, but only from your own perspective. This time try to ask yourself if there is anything you are doing which may be contributing to the problem.

If your answer is "No," then you are not being honest with yourself. Most likely there is something, however small it may be, that you are contributing to the problem. It doesn't mean that you are to blame or that the problem is all your fault. But it does mean that most marital problems are caused by a *cholent* of factors, at least some of which are contributed by each spouse.

Once your answer is "Yes," make an effort to improve yourself. Even if you believe that your spouse is mostly to blame, try to change yourself first. It really is easier than trying to change someone else.

Now, if you've tried unsuccessfully to discuss the problem with your spouse, and if you've tried to improve yourself and the situation has still not gotten better, then you really should seek outside help.

What about trying again, before going for outside help? There certainly is no harm in trying again once, twice or even three times. But to continuously repeat unsuccessful efforts is worse than just not helping; it is destructive. In other words, once you see that your efforts are failing, do not persist with the same strategies that have proven ineffective in the past.

 **Yossi** and **Leah** made this mistake and it almost cost them their marriage. Soon after their wedding, Yossi couldn't help noticing Leah's thinly veiled resentment towards him. It came out in almost every other interchange between them. Leah was short-tempered, impatient and at times openly hostile towards Yossi.

The tension between Yossi and Leah continued for many years and grew progressively more intense. As the children got older, they became a focal point of conflict, because Yossi and Leah differed sharply on most parenting issues.

Both Leah and Yossi acknowledged to themselves and to each other that there were serious problems in the marriage. Whenever they tried to discuss the problems, however, the discussion itself would lead to an argument.

Yossi and Leah failed to resolve their differences during these discussions because they both broke all three cardinal rules outlined earlier. It didn't even matter who started. Sometimes it was Yossi who would exaggerate by asking Leah why she "always" or "never" did this or that. Sometimes it was Leah who would bring in unrelated, tangential issues, such as, "Oh, I do, huh? Then tell me, why was it two weeks ago that *you*...?!" And each one always assumed he "understood" what the other really meant, really felt or really wanted, without having to ask for clarification.

Clearly, these discussions resolved nothing. They succeeded only in generating massive bitterness, frustration and resentment.

Surprisingly, however, it took almost twelve years until Yossi and Leah decided to get outside help. By that time, they were both feeling so hopeless and alienated that divorce began to look like a viable alternative. Why did they wait so long?

Neither Leah nor Yossi really pushed to get outside help. This was one of the few issues upon which they agreed. Their resistance to outside help was based on two factors. First, they would have had to admit their own failures. Even though their marriage was anything but successful, as long as they were not getting outside help they could delude themselves into thinking that things were not really that bad. This was similar to the attitude of some people who believe that if you avoid seeing a physician, you're not really sick, in spite of whatever symptoms you have.

The second cause for their delay in seeking help was their mistaken belief in the efficacy of their problem solving. They each believed that they were correct about the causes and solutions to their problems. Why hadn't it worked up until now? Because they simply hadn't tried *hard* enough. Maybe next time, Yossi thought, I'll be able to explain to Leah why she is wrong. Perhaps another time, Leah reasoned to herself, I'll succeed in showing Yossi how foolish he is.

Yossi and Leah could each be compared to someone eagerly trying to enter a locked door. Standing at the door with a key-chain full of keys, this individual tries one key in the lock. When that key fails to open the door, the person desperately jiggles and plays with the key again and again. Instead of trying another key, this person stubbornly tries the same key, over and over. After all, he reassures himself, this *must* be the right key.

Had Yossi and Leah given up on their "keys" earlier, perhaps they would have been spared some of their twelve years of anguish and suffering.

Once you have made the decision that outside help is needed to unlock the door to your *shalom bayis*, the next question you may ask is: "Where can I go for help." The answer to that question is the subject of the next chapter.

# CHAPTER EIGHT

# Where and How to Get Help

## Where to Get Help

As mentioned in chapter 6, your parents should not be your first choice for outside help. Certainly they care greatly for you, your welfare and your happiness. But they are too close to you to be able to remain truly impartial and objective. Therefore, your first choice should be a *gadol* who can bring the wisdom of *da'as Torah* and years of experience to bear in helping you solve your problem.

The *rav* you turn to need not be a *gadol hador*. Furthermore, he does not have to be famous or politically influential. But he should be respected by both you and your spouse.

Suppose there is no one "available." The *rav* you know best is out of town for an extended period. The *rav* you respect most is not acceptable to your spouse. Or, the *rav* you both agree to see has no time to meet with you. Where else can you go to get help?

There are really many people who are qualified to advise you and your spouse on alternative methods to solve your marital problems. Without mentioning names, of course, a few suggestions can be made.

— Your former *rosh yeshiva*. You may not have kept up your ties with the *rosh yeshiva* of the yeshiva you used to attend. Nevertheless, he most probably still remembers you and would be willing to meet you and your wife.

— The *chassidishe rebbe* in your town or neighborhood. You may not consider yourself one of his *chassidim*, and you may not even feel "chassidicly inclined." Nevertheless, that should not deter you from seeking guidance from someone whose *ahavas Yisrael* knows no categorical boundaries.

— Your former *menahel*. It has been many years since you graduated high school and seminary. But the *menahel* you admired so much then is probably still in charge of the same institution. You can expect him to show you and your husband the same courtesy and consideration he showed you in the past.

— The *rav* of the *shul* you attend on Shabbos. When he is delivering sermons or *shiurim*, he may not seem like someone who could help with marital problems. Nevertheless, your *rav* probably has years of experience dealing with problems similar to yours. Don't worry; if he does not feel qualified to help you, he will tell you.

What about "professional" help? Should you ever consult with a marriage counselor or therapist? Is it better to go to an agency or to someone in private practice? Does it make any difference if the therapist is a psychologist, a social worker or a psychiatrist? How do you know if the counselor is properly trained, licensed and qualified? How do you know if the counselor is effective, compassionate, and understanding? Does the therapist have to be Orthodox?

These are only some of the questions people ask about professional help. They are all important questions which need to be asked. The answers, however, must be individualized. In other words, what is right for one couple may not be right for another couple. In addition, general answers to these questions could lead to even further confusion.

Therefore, if you are concerned about whether or not

to seek professional help, first consult with a *rav*. If he agrees that professional help is necessary, he will be able to guide you to a professional who is right for you. After all, you are not interested in conducting a survey. What you want is the *one* therapist who will help you solve your problems. By getting a referral from a *rav* you are taking advantage of his previous experience with many other couples.

It may even surprise you to learn that the *rav* has referred other people for professional help in the past. Sometimes it is a well-kept secret and for good reasons. But the fact is that almost *every rosh yeshiva, chassidishe rebbe, menahel* and *shul rav* has the telephone number of at least one therapist to whom he has referred others before. Most likely, the *rav, menahel, rebbe* or *rosh yeshiva* got some feedback from the experiences of others with that therapist. The referral, then, will not be made solely on the basis of reputation. You may even hear some reassurance such as, "I've sent other people to her in the past, and they were always quite satisfied."

Selecting a therapist on your own is at best a risky affair. At worst, it is dangerous. If you are too embarrassed to ask your *rosh yeshiva, rebbe, menahel* or *rav* for a referral, you can call him up on the phone. You don't have to give your name and even if you do, you can just say you are calling for a friend.

Once you have decided that you need outside help, one final question arises: how should you go about arranging for the help you need?

## How to Get Help

To some people, the question of how to get help is superfluous. They feel that only "common sense" is needed in order to understand the procedures involved in seeking help.

Nevertheless, as stated earlier, since we live in an age when so much that is obvious gets overlooked, a brief outline of the recommended procedure will be presented here.

— First, you should inform your spouse of your conclusion that outside help is needed. This may come as a shock to him. If so, that should indicate to you that your spouse has not understood how much you have been bothered and upset by the marital problems. Sometimes that shock alone can break up the logjam of blocked communication. Countless initial consultations for professional marital counseling, for example, have been canceled in advance just because the setting of the appointment itself was sufficient to bring about change.

It is also possible that your spouse will have the opposite reaction. He may be quite relieved to hear that you want to get outside help. Your spouse may have secretly wanted the same thing but was afraid to suggest it.

Regardless of your spouse's initial reaction, you need to inform him of your desire to seek outside help for another very important reason.

— You must include your spouse in the process of deciding with whom you should consult. Of course, your spouse may want no part of this and may flatly refuse to participate. Nevertheless, you stand the greatest chance of getting your spouse to come with you if you include him in the selection process.

If, on the other hand, you simply announce to your spouse that you have decided that Rabbi so-and-so must be consulted, your spouse may feel outnumbered. He may suspect that you have chosen this *rav* because you believe he will be more partial to you. If your spouse has an equal say regarding who should be consulted, then you remove at least one barrier to his participation.

Right now, you may feel a strong preference to meet with the *rav* alone, without informing your spouse. That may provide you with some temporary relief. But if you ever hope to iron out your differences with your spouse, both of you will have to be involved in the process, at some point.

Then call just to make an appointment. Don't go into any details over the phone. Trying to prejudice the *rav* in advance will be futile and perhaps even counterproductive.

From here on, follow the *rav*'s advice and recommendations. He may want to see you both together first. Or, he may prefer to meet you each individually. Either way, you should try to cooperate with his approach. Just remember, you are not the first couple he has counseled.

What if your spouse refuses to cooperate with any outside help? She is so firmly convinced that it is all your fault that she feels it is unnecessary to participate in the process. You are simply told, "You go, yourself! After all, you're the one who's got to straighten out, not me!" Or, you may be told that your problems are a private matter which should not be discussed with anyone outside of the marriage. Another possibility is that you are told that the only *rav* your spouse will speak with is Rabbi so-and-so who lives in Australia and can only be reached by phone on the last Thursday of each month from 3 to 4 A.M.

No matter what you are told, if your spouse refuses to cooperate, ignore all protestations. Make the selection yourself and then call for an individual appointment with the *rav* of your choosing. Be sure to let your spouse know when and where the appointment is scheduled. You would be amazed how many reluctant spouses show up for these appointments when they see that you "really mean business."

But suppose you know that your spouse would never join you to meet with any *rav*, whatsoever? Is it still advisable to arrange for an individual meeting?

The answer is a resounding "Yes!" There are a few

good reasons why you should make and keep this individual appointment with the *rav*, even if your spouse does not show up.

First, your spouse may be willing to participate later, after you have already initiated the process of seeking help. Sometimes the husband or wife wants to hear a report of what transpired at the first meeting. If so, respectfully decline to give your spouse a transcript of your meeting. Tactfully and courteously tell your spouse that if she wants to know what is being discussed, she will have to come along for the next meeting.

But even if your spouse will never, ever join you to meet with the *rav*, your individual meeting can still be beneficial. You may be able to get valuable advice regarding how to handle and deal with your spouse. The problems may not be resolved completely, but at least you will not feel so helpless.

Finally, seeking outside help over the objections of your spouse automatically reestablishes your marital relationship on a new foundation. If your spouse is the type of person who will stubbornly refuse to meet with any *rav* and forbids you to do so, you may have been suffering in a very imbalanced relationship. Your spouse could only make such a stubborn refusal if she really believed that you could be so easily controlled.

In reality, of course, each spouse retains his own individuality and autonomy even after marriage. If this truism has been obscured in your marriage, you may have assumed such a passive role that you contributed to your own victimization. When you take the strong, unilateral step of going to consult with a *rav*, on your own, you dramatically reverse the imbalance in your relationship. You demonstrate to your spouse that you are not under his or her total control. Even if it does not result in any positive changes in your spouse, it will do wonders to build your self-esteem and confidence, which in turn can eventually improve your chances of successfully dealing with your spouse.

Hopefully, you will never need to apply the advice of this chapter to your personal life. Hopefully, you will be so well prepared and so well suited to your spouse that you will never need to seek any outside help.

But even if you never need help, it is most unlikely that you will never come across another married couple who does need help. So when you realize that your married friends or relatives could benefit from outside help, what can you do? The next chapter answers this question.

# CHAPTER NINE

# When They Need Help

## What You Should Not Do

Before getting into what you can do to help your friends or relatives with marital problems, what you should not do must be clarified. First and foremost, you should not take sides in any marital dispute. This does not mean that you should not listen, patiently and sympathetically. What it does mean is that you must suspend your judgment as to who is at fault. You are probably going to have greater access to one side or the other; and since you won't get *both* sides equally, you should avoid this first pitfall of taking sides.

Next, you should not try to conduct marriage counseling. Marriage counseling is a tricky, complex and serious endeavor which should be left to those with more experience. It may look easy to you. Believe me; it is not. Therefore, you could ultimately do more harm than good by trying to use "common sense" when more effective methods are required.

Finally, you should not offer any false reassurance. When someone presents a problem to you which is overwhelming him, your natural desire is to want to calm him down. But if you try to reassure someone that the situation will probably improve *when you are not certain that it will*, you are offering false reassurance. People who receive this kind of premature encouragement generally either feel that you really don't understand how serious the problem is or they feel great disappointment later when your promises don't come true.

## What You Can Do

Now we can discuss what you can do to help a friend or relative with a marital problem. You can encourage them to seek outside help.

You need not begin with advice to the couple to sit down and discuss the problem with each other (as suggested in chapter 7) because by the time you are made aware of the difficulty, that approach has probably failed, been ruled out, or both. The very fact that you are made aware of the problem directly or indirectly is a good indication itself that outside help is already needed.

How should you present this to the individual or couple involved? The best way to recommend outside help is to be direct and get straight to the point. For example, "You really seem to be having a rough time and I certainly do not feel competent to advise you on these matters. Perhaps you should consult with a *rav*."

Won't the person feel put off or insulted? Not necessarily. In fact the individual who is suffering and upset may be relieved to hear that someone is finally taking the matter seriously.

Is there anything else that can be done for a friend or relative with a marital problem, besides recommending outside help? What your friend or relative may need more than the recommendation is help in carrying it out. In other words, your friend may need to discuss with you the whole issue of seeking outside help. So you can do a lot for your friend by listening to his concerns, apprehensions and hesitations about getting outside help. If you hear your friend out and respond appropriately you will be providing a service that no marriage counselor, professional or *rav*, can provide: helping someone overcome their resistance to outside support. After all, by the time people do come for marriage counseling they have already made up their minds that it is necessary!

In order to help people overcome their resistance to outside assistance, you need to familiarize yourself with the most common objections. Suggested responses to these objections will be included in the following hypothetical dialogue.

*Friend*: I just can't take it anymore. She is just impossible. You wouldn't believe what happened last night!

*You*: I realize you're having a rough time, but I don't believe that I'm the one to help you. Have you considered consulting a *rav*?

*Friend*: Oh, what good would that do? She won't listen to anyone, anyway. She always thinks she's right.

*You*: Even if she won't listen, you may get some good advice about how to handle the situation.

*Friend*: I really don't know any *rabbanim* who I would feel comfortable discussing this problem with.

*You*: Why don't you try Rav Schwartz? I believe he has a lot of experience with *shalom bayis* cases.

*Friend*: I'd be be too embarrassed to speak with him. Someone might see me there and suspect I have a marriage problem. I don't want anyone to know.

*You*:    Why don't you call Rav Schwartz on the phone? Maybe you wouldn't have to see him at all.

*Friend*:    Somehow, I'm afraid she would be able to fool Rav Schwartz by coming across in such a friendly, compassionate manner. She can do that, you know. That's how I fell into this marriage in the first place!

*You*:    If you're not satisfied with what Rav Schwartz tells you, you certainly don't have to continue with him. Just because you consult with him once puts you under no obligation.

*Friend*:    What if he can't handle my problem and wants to refer me to a professional? I'd feel I'd have to go. Even if I were referred by Rav Schwartz, I don't feel I could trust a professional. I've heard such horror stories. Who knows what might happen?!

This final objection is shared by a lot of people. Any reassurance coming from a professional could, of course, be suspect. Therefore, I would like to address this concern by quoting from a letter sent to me by a woman I interviewed for a research project I was conducting on the attitudes of Orthodox people concerning professional help. (The Meaning of the Therapist's Religious Identity to Orthodox Jewish Clients, University Microfilms, Ann Arbor, Mich., 1983).

Dear Dr. Wikler,
   Apropos of our meeting last week, several things occurred to me and I think they may be relevant to your study....

Many people distrust therapy because they are afraid that a therapist can have too profound an influence on his client... What has gotten back to me recently is that some people have been saying that my wanting a divorce is the fault of my therapist — that he led me into it. These people have never met nor spoken with him, nor have they ever heard about my therapy from me. All they know is that I am in therapy.

What disturbs me most about this is that I can just hear them telling the next woman in distress: "I know a case where a couple got divorced only because the therapist pushed her into it. Keep away from professional help. It's dangerous!"...

These people are passing judgment without even the most rudimentary understanding of what therapy is....

It seems to me so unfair (to therapists as well as the community-in-need at large) to pass judgment on and censor something one knows virtually nothing about. Professional counseling is fighting a losing battle to prove its value to the *frum* community if it will not even be judged on the basis of what it is, rather than on conjecture and distortion.

I wish you much *hatzlacha* on this research of yours.

Sincerely,
Mrs. Cohen

In the final analysis, of course, there really is no way to get people to accept outside help if they are totally opposed to it. (See *Taanis*, 7a for Rebbe Chanina bar Poppa's exposition of *Yeshaya* 55:1, "*kol tsomai l'chu lamayim*," which could apply here as well.) But don't feel defeated. They simply may not be ready now. In a little while, if things do not improve, who knows, they may just call Rav Schwartz, after all.

# CHAPTER TEN

# A Closing Word

*And Yaakov worked seven years for Rachel, and they seemed in his
eyes like a few days because of his love for her.* (*Beraishis* 29:20)

When we approach this verse from our own frame of
reference, it appears anomalous. If Yaakov Avinu really
loved Rachel Imainu, then the seven years should have felt
more like seven *hundred* years. Why does the Torah tell us
that Yaakov viewed the seven-year delay in being able to
marry Rachel as if it were only a few days?

The Dubno Maggid, Rabbi Yaakov ben Zeev Kranz
(1741-1804), answered this question as follows. There are
two types of desire. The first type of desire is an instinctual
drive for pleasure. Someone motivated by this type of
desire seeks immediate gratification and becomes frustrated with even the slightest delay. The second type of
desire is a rational plan for future benefits. Someone motivated by this type of desire is willing to delay gratification
in order to carefully execute his long-range plans.

According to the Dubno Maggid, therefore, Yaakov
was not seeking to marry Rachel in order to gratify instinctual drives for immediate pleasure. Rather, he was motivated by a purely rational plan to establish a family that
would eventually become the nation of *Klal Yisrael.* Since
he saw his marriage as part of the long-range plan for the
destiny of the Jewish people, Yaakov was able to cope so

well with the seven-year wait that it felt to him like a few days.

But doesn't the Torah state that Yaakov "loved" Rachel? Why didn't that love make him more uncomfortable with the delay instead of making is easier?

Again, the Dubno Maggid clarifies this verse. If someone is fond of a particular food, why does he eat it? Generally, we would say that he loves that item. But in reality, he does not love the food. He loves himself and that is why he eats it.

Yaakov's love for Rachel was not a selfish love through which Yaakov sought to gratify his own personal desires. As the Torah states, "He loved her," not for how she could please him but for what they could build and accomplish in life together.

The message of the Dubno Maggid to us, then, is clear. If you approach marriage impulsively, out of a selfish desire to gratify your love of yourself, your marriage will fall short of its Divinely ordained potential. But if you approach marriage with a thoughtful, level-headed desire to build a Jewish home, then you will become a partner with Yaakov Avinu and Rachel Imainu.

This applies not only to those who approach marriage as they walk down the aisle to their *chuppa* but also to those who approach the rest of their marriage with years of married life behind them. Let us all hope and pray that every Jewish couple will follow the examples set by Yaakov and Rachel — that they will prepare themselves for unselfish devotion to the sanctity of their relationship and that they will build a home which can serve as a proper foundation for future generations of *Klal Yisrael*, an everlasting Jewish home, *a bayis ne'eman b'Yisrael, Amen.*

# Glossary

The following glossary provides a partial explanation of some of the Hebrew and Yiddish (Y.) words and phrases used in this book. The spelling and explanations reflect the way the specific word is used herein. Often, there are alternate spellings and meanings for the words.

ADAM HARISHON: the first man, created by God.

A GUTTEN TAG: (Y.) "Have a good day."

AHAVAS YISRAEL: love of one's fellow Jew.

AIYDLE: (Y.) refined.

AMEN: response to a blessing or prayer, meaning either "it is true" or "so be it."

ASSUR: forbidden by Jewish law.

AVINU: our father.

BACHUR(IM): a young unmarried man.

BARUCH HASHEM: "Thank God."

BAYIS NE'EMAN B'YISRAEL: everlasting Jewish home.

BEN TORAH (BNAI TORAH): learned, observant Jew.

BERAISHIS: the Book of Genesis.

BESHERT: (Y.) ordained in Heaven.

B'EZRAS HASHEM: "with the help of God."

BIMHAIRA BIYAMAINU: "speedily and in our days."

BUBBIES: (Y.) (pl.) grandmothers.

CHASSAN: bridegroom.

CHASSIDIM: (pl.) followers of Chassidism, a religious and social movement founded by Rabbi Israel Baal Shem Tov in the eighteenth century.

CHASSIDISHE REBBE: (Y.) leader of a group of chassidim.

CHAS V'SHALOM: Heaven forbid.

CHAVRUSA (CHAVRUSOS): study partner.

CHAVURA: close-knit group.

CHAZAL: Sages of the Talmud.

CHESSED: kindness.

CHUMASH: the Pentateuch.

CHINNUCH: education in Jewish observance.

CHUMRA: stringent practice.

CHUPPA: wedding canopy.

DA'AS TORAH: the accepted, Torah-based opinions of recognized rabbinic authorities.

ERETZ YISRAEL: the Land of Israel.

FRUM: (Y.) religious.

GADOL (GEDOLIM): great Torah sage and leader.

GADOL HADOR (GEDOLAI HADOR): great Torah sage and leader of the generation.

GEMARA: Talmud.

GET: divorce executed in accordance with Jewish law.

HAGGADA: the story of the Jews' redemption from Egypt, read on Passover during the seder.

HALACHA (HALACHOS): Jewish law.

HASHEM: God.

HATZLACHA: success.

IMAINU: our mother.

KALLA: bride.

KASHRUS: Jewish dietary laws.

KAVOD SHAMAYIM: the glory of Heaven.

KESUBA: Jewish marriage contract.

KIRUV: bringing non- or less observant Jews closer to Torah observance.

KLAL YISRAEL: the people of Israel.

KOLLEL: talmudical academy for married men.

LAMDAN: Torah scholar possessing an in-depth knowledge of the Talmud.

L'CHAYIM: "to life"; a toast made in celebration of a happy occasion.

MASHGIACH (MASHGICHIM): supervisor.

MASHGIACH RUCHANI: spiritual guide and counselor of a yeshiva.

MASHIACH TZIDKAINU: "the Messiah, our righteous one."

MECHANAICH (MECHANCHIM): educator

MECHILLA: forgiveness.

MENAHEL: principal.

MINHAG: custom.

MINYAN: quorum of ten men necessary for communal prayer.

MITZVA: commandment.

MOTZA'AI SHABBOS: Saturday evening after the conclusion of the Sabbath.

NESHAMA: soul.

NISSAYON: test.

POSAIK ACHARON: final halachic authority.

RABBANIM: (pl.) rabbis.

RAV: rabbi.

REBBE (REBBE'IM): (Y.) rabbi and teacher.

REBBETZIN: (Y.) the wife of a rabbi.

ROSH YESHIVA (ROSHAI YESHIVA): the dean of a Torah academy.

SCHMUESIM: (Y.) (pl.) lectures, usually on Torah ethics.

SEDER: a fixed period of time set aside for Torah study.

SHADCHAN: (Y.) matchmaker.

SHALOM BAYIS: marital tranquility.

SHANA RISHONA: the first year of marriage.

SHAS: Talmud.

SH'CHINA: the presence of God in the world.

SHE'AILA (SHE'AILOS): question arising in Jewish law.

SHEVA BRACHOS: a festive meal given for newlyweds during the first week after their wedding; at the conclusion of this meal, seven blessings are recited.

SHIDDUCH(IM): (Y.) arranged match.

SHITTA: position.

SHIUR(IM): Torah lecture.
SHMOS: the Book of Exodus.
SHOMRAI MITZVOS: observers of Jewish law and tradition.
SHUL: (Y.) synagogue.
SIMCHA: joy.

TALMID(IM): student.
TALMID CHACHAM: Torah scholar.
TESHUVOS: rabbinic responsa.
TZNIUS: modesty.

VAAD(IM): committee.
VAYIKRA: the Book of Leviticus.

YAISH ME'AYIN: creation ex nihilo.
YAITZER HARA: evil inclination.
YAITZER HATOV: good inclination.
YESHIVA: a Torah academy.
YOM TOV: a Jewish holiday.

ZAIDIES: (Y.) (pl.) grandfathers.
ZMAN: period of Torah study, in a yeshiva or kollel, lasting several weeks or several months.